TOUCHSTONE

SECOND EDITION

STUDENT'S BOOK 1A

MICHAEL MCCARTHY

JEANNE MCCARTEN

HELEN SANDIFORD

CAMBRIDGE
UNIVERSITY PRESS

Shaftesbury Road, Cambridge CB2 8EA, United Kingdom

One Liberty Plaza, 20th Floor, New York, NY 10006, USA

477 Williamstown Road, Port Melbourne, VIC 3207, Australia

314–321, 3rd Floor, Plot 3, Splendor Forum, Jasola District Centre,
New Delhi – 110025, India

103 Penang Road, #05–06/07, Visioncrest Commercial, Singapore 238467

Cambridge University Press & Assessment is a department of the University of Cambridge.

We share the University's mission to contribute to society through the pursuit of education, learning and research at the highest international levels of excellence.

www.cambridge.org
Information on this title: www.cambridge.org/9781107627925

© Cambridge University Press & Assessment 2005, 2014

First published 2005
Second edition 2014

20 19 18 17 16

Printed in Malaysia by Vivar Printing

A catalogue record for this publication is available from the British Library

ISBN 978-1-107-67987-0 Student's Book
ISBN 978-1-107-62792-5 Student's Book A
ISBN 978-1-107-65345-0 Student's Book B
ISBN 978-1-107-63933-1 Workbook
ISBN 978-1-107-67071-6 Workbook A
ISBN 978-1-107-69125-4 Workbook B
ISBN 978-1-107-68330-3 Full Contact
ISBN 978-1-107-66769-3 Full Contact A
ISBN 978-1-107-61366-9 Full Contact B
ISBN 978-1-107-64223-2 Teacher's Edition with Assessment Audio CD/CD-ROM
ISBN 978-1-107-61414-7 Class Audio CDs (4)

Additional resources for this publication at www.cambridge.org/touchstone2

Acknowledgments

Touchstone Second Edition has benefited from extensive development research. The authors and publishers would like to extend their thanks to the following reviewers and consultants for their valuable insights and suggestions:

Ana Lúcia da Costa Maia de Almeida and Mônica da Costa Monteiro de Souza from **IBEU**, Rio de Janeiro, Brazil; Andreza Cristiane Melo do Lago from **Magic English School,** Manaus, Brazil; Magaly Mendes Lemos from **ICBEU**, São José dos Campos, Brazil; Maria Lucia Zaorob, São Paulo, Brazil; Patricia McKay Aronis from **CEL LEP**, São Paulo, Brazil; Carlos Gontow, São Paulo, Brazil; Christiane Augusto Gomes da Silva from **Colégio Visconde de Porto Seguro,** São Paulo, Brazil; Silvana Fontana from **Lord's Idiomas**, São Paulo, Brazil; Alexander Fabiano Morishigue from **Speed Up Idiomas**, Jales, Brazil; Elisabeth Blom from **Casa Thomas Jefferson**, Brasília, Brazil; Michelle Dear from **International Academy of English**, Toronto, ON, Canada; Walter Duarte Marin, Laura Hurtado Portela, Jorge Quiroga, and Ricardo Suarez, from **Centro Colombo Americano**, Bogotá, Colombia; Jhon Jairo Castaneda Macias from **Praxis English Academy**, Bucaramanga, Colombia; Gloria Liliana Moreno Vizcaino from **Universidad Santo Tomas**, Bogotá, Colombia; Elizabeth Ortiz from **Copol English Institute (COPEI)**, Guayaquil, Ecuador; Henry Foster from **Kyoto Tachibana University,** Kyoto, Japan; Steven Kirk from **Tokyo University**, Tokyo, Japan; J. Lake from **Fukuoka Woman's University**, Fukuoka, Japan; Etsuko Yoshida from **Mie University**, Mie, Japan; B. Bricklin Zeff from **Hokkai Gakuen University**, Hokkaido, Japan; Ziad Abu-Hamatteh from **Al-Balqa' Applied University**, Al-Salt, Jordan; Roxana Pérez Flores from **Universidad Autonoma de Coahuila Language Center**, Saltillo, Mexico; Kim Alejandro Soriano Jimenez from **Universidad Politecnica de Altamira**, Altamira, Mexico; Tere Calderon Rosas from **Universidad Autonoma Metropolitana Campus Iztapalapa**, Mexico City, Mexico; Lilia Bondareva, Polina Ermakova, and Elena Frumina, from **National Research Technical University MISiS**, Moscow, Russia; Dianne C. Ellis from **Kyung Hee University**, Gyeonggi-do, South Korea; Jason M. Ham and Victoria Jo from **Institute of Foreign Language Education, Catholic University of Korea**, Gyeonggi-do, South Korea; Shaun Manning from **Hankuk University of Foreign Studies**, Seoul, South Korea; Natalie Renton from **Busan National University of Education**, Busan, South Korea; Chris Soutter from **Busan University of Foreign Studies**, Busan, South Korea; Andrew Cook from **Dong A University**, Busan, South Korea; Raymond Wowk from **Daejin University**, Gyeonggi-do, South Korea; Ming-Hui Hsieh and Jessie Huang from **National Central University**, Zhongli, Taiwan; Kim Phillips from **Chinese Culture University**, Taipei, Taiwan; Alex Shih from **China University of Technology**, Taipei Ta-Liao Township, Taiwan; Porntip Bodeepongse from **Thaksin University**, Songkhla, Thailand; Nattaya Puakpong and Pannathon Sangarun from **Suranaree University of Technology**, Nakhon Ratchasima, Thailand; Barbara Richards, Gloria Stewner-Manzanares, and Caroline Thompson, from **Montgomery College**, Rockville, MD, USA; Kerry Vrabel from **Gateway Community College**, Phoenix, AZ, USA.

Touchstone Second Edition authors and publishers would also like to thank the following individuals and institutions who have provided excellent feedback and support on *Touchstone Blended*:

Gordon Lewis, Vice President, Laureate Languages and Chris Johnson, Director, Laureate English Programs, Latin America from **Laureate International Universities**; **Universidad de las Americas**, Santiago, Chile; **University of Victoria**, Paris, France; **Universidad Technólogica Centroamericana**, Honduras; **Instititut Universitaire de Casablanca**, Morocco; **Universidad Peruana de Ciencias Aplicadas**, Lima, Peru; **CIBERTEC**, Peru; **National Research Technical University (MiSIS)**, Moscow, Russia; **Institut Obert de Catalunya (IOC)**, Barcelona, Spain; Sedat Çilingir, Burcu Tezcan, and Didem Mutçalıoğlu from **İstanbul Bilgi Üniversitesi**, Istanbul, Turkey.

Touchstone Second Edition authors and publishers would also like to thank the following contributors to *Touchstone Second Edition*:

Sue Aldcorn, Frances Amrani, Deborah Gordon, Lisa Hutchins, Nancy Jordan, Steven Kirk, Genevieve Kocienda, Linda-Marie Koza, Geraldine Mark, Julianna Nielsen, Kathryn O'Dell, Nicola Prentis, Ellen Shaw, Kristin Sherman, Luis Silva Susa, Mary Vaughn, Kerry S. Vrabel, Shari Young and Eric Zuarino.

Authors' Acknowledgments

The authors would like to thank all the Cambridge University Press staff and freelancers who were involved in the creation of *Touchstone Second Edition*. In addition, they would like to acknowledge a huge debt of gratitude that they owe to two people: Mary Vaughn, for her role in creating *Touchstone First Edition* and for being a constant source of wisdom ever since, and Bryan Fletcher, who also had the vision that has led to the success of *Touchstone Blended Learning*.

Helen Sandiford would like to thank her family for their love and support, especially her husband Bryan.

The author team would also like to thank each other, for the joy of working together, sharing the same professional dedication, and for the mutual support and friendship.

Finally, the authors would like to thank our dear friend Alejandro Martinez, Global Training Manager, who sadly passed away in 2012. He is greatly missed by all who had the pleasure to work with him. Alex was a huge supporter of *Touchstone* and everyone is deeply grateful to him for his contribution to its success.

Touchstone Level 1A Contents and learning outcomes

Interaction	Skills				Self study
Conversation strategies	**Listening**	**Reading**	**Writing**	**Free talk**	**Vocabulary notebook**
• Ask *How about you?* • Use everyday expressions like *Yeah* and *Thanks*	• Recognize responses to *hello* and *good-bye* ***Memberships*** • Listen for personal information, and complete application forms	• Different types of identification cards and documents	• Complete an application	***The name game*** • Group work: Play a game to learn classmates' names	***Meetings and greetings*** • Write new expressions with their responses
• Ask for help in class • Respond to *Thank you* and *I'm sorry*	***Who's absent today?*** • Listen to a classroom conversation, and say where students are ***Following instructions*** • Recognize classroom instructions	• Classroom conversations	• Write questions about locations	***What do you remember?*** • Pair work: Look at a picture and list what you remember	***My things*** • Link things with places
• Show interest by repeating information and asking questions • Use *Really?* to show interest or surprise	***Friends*** • Listen to three people's descriptions of their friends, and fill in the missing words	• A family tree	• Write questions about people	***Guess the famous person*** • Pair work: Ask *yes-no* questions to guess a famous person	***All in the family*** • Make a family tree
Checkpoint Units 1–3 pages 31–32					
• Say more than *yes* or *no* when you answer a question • Start answers with *Well* if you need time to think or if the answer isn't a simple yes or no	***Casual conversations*** • Listen and match the correct response ***Teen habits*** • Listen to an interview with an average American teenager	***Are you like an average American?*** • Read an article about the habits of an average American	***A typical week*** • Write about a classmate's typical week for a class website • Use capital letters and periods	***Do you have the same media habits?*** • Pair work: Compare media habits with young adults in the United States	***Verbs, verbs, verbs*** • Draw and label simple pictures of new vocabulary
• Ask questions in two ways to be clear and not too direct • Use *I mean* to repeat your ideas or to say more	***What do they say next?*** • Listen and guess the questions people answer ***Using phones*** • Listen to how people use their cell phones	***Do You Need a Technology diet?*** • Read an article about technology addicts	***Technology and you*** • Write a reply to an email asking for technology advice • Link ideas with *and* and *but*	***Favorite free-time activities*** • Pair work: Make guesses about a classmate's free-time activities	***Do what? Go where?*** • Write verbs with the words you use after them
• Use *Me too* or *Me neither* to show things in common • Respond with *Right* or *I know* to agree or show you are listening	***What's on this weekend?*** • Listen to a radio show for times and places of events ***Where to go?*** • Listen for decisions made in conversations, then react to statements	***The Village*** • Read a travel guide to New York	***City guide*** • Write a city guide • Use prepositions for time and place: *between through, at, on, for,* and *from . . . to . . .*	***Find the difference*** • Pair work: List the differences between two neighborhoods	***A time and a place . . .*** • Link times of day with activities
Checkpoint Units 4–6 pages 63–64					

Useful language for . . .

Getting help

What's the word for "_____" in English?

How do you spell "_____"?

What does "_____" mean?

I'm sorry. Can you repeat that, please?

Can you say that again, please?

Can you explain the activity again, please?

Working with a partner

I'm ready. Are you ready?

No. Just a minute.

You go first.

OK. I'll go first.

What do you have for number 1?

I have . . .

Do you want to be A or B?

I'll be A. You can be B.

Let's do the activity again.

OK. Let's change roles.

That's it. We're finished.

What do we do next?

Can I read your paragraph?

Sure. Here you go.

All about you

✓ Can Do! In this unit, you learn how to . . .

Lesson A
- Say *hello* and *good-bye*
- Introduce yourself

Lesson B
- Ask for, give, and spell names
- Use the verb *be* with *I*, *we*, and *you*

Lesson C
- Exchange email addresses, phone numbers, etc.
- Complete an application form

Lesson D
- Ask *How about you?*
- Use expressions like *Thanks* or *Thank you*

Before you begin . . .

Match each expression with a picture.

- ☐ Good night.
- ☐ Thanks.
- ☐ Good morning.
- ☐ Hi.
- 1 Bye.
- ☐ Hello.
- ☐ Thank you.
- ☐ Good-bye.

1 Getting started

A Look at the photos. Guess the words in the conversations. Check (✓) the boxes.

☐ Good-bye.　　☐ Hello.　　☐ Thanks.　　☐ Hi.　　☐ Good morning.

B 🔊 1.02 Listen. Are Matt and Sarah friends? How about Rob and Sandra? Practice the conversations.

Matt	Good morning, Sarah. How are you?
Sarah	Good. How are you, Matt?
Matt	I'm fine, thanks.

Rob	Hello. I'm Rob Jones.
Sandra	Hi, I'm Sandra Davis. Nice to meet you.
Rob	Nice to meet you.

Figure it out **C** Can you complete these conversations? Use the conversations above to help you. Then practice with a partner. Use your own names.

These people are friends:

1. A Hi, Pat. How ___*are*___ you?
   B I'm fine. How are you?
   A Good, _____ .

2. A Good _____ , Anna.
   B Hi, Dan. _____ are you?
   A I'm _____ , thanks.

These people meet for the first time:

3. A Hello. _____ Chris Evans.
   B Hi. I'm Grace Song.
   A _____ to meet you, Grace.

4. A Hello. I'm Sarah.
   B Nice to meet _____ . I'm Alan.
   A Nice to _____ you.

2 Building vocabulary

A 🔊 1.03 **Listen. Are these people saying "hello" or "good-bye"? Practice the conversations.**

Emily	Good night.
Shawn	Good night. Have a good evening.
Emily	Thank you. You too.

Tom	Bye. See you tomorrow.
Rita	Bye. See you.

B 🔊 1.04 **Read the conversations and check (✓) the correct responses. Listen and check your answers. Then practice with a partner.**

1. Good-bye. Have a nice evening.
   - ☐ Thank you. You too.
   - ☐ Good, thanks.

2. Hey, Oscar. How are you?
   - ☐ Good, thanks.
   - ☐ See you tomorrow.

3. See you later.
   - ☐ Thanks. You too.
   - ☐ OK. Have a good day.

4. Hello. I'm Emma.
   - ☐ See you later.
   - ☐ Nice to meet you.

5. Good morning.
   - ☐ Hi. How are you?
   - ☐ Bye. See you.

6. Good night. Have a good weekend.
   - ☐ Good. How are you?
   - ☐ Bye. See you next week.

Word sort **C** **Look at the conversations above. Which expressions mean "hello"? Which expressions mean "good-bye"? Complete the chart.**

"Hello"	"Good-bye"
	Good night

📙 **Vocabulary notebook** p. 10

D **Class activity** Say "hello" and "good-bye" to five classmates using the expressions above.

1 Saying names in English

A 🔊 1.05 Listen to these people give their names. Then complete the information.

❸ Hello. I'm Ana Sanchez. My **first name** is Maria. Ana is my **middle name**.

❷ Hi. My name is Don. My **full name** is Don Allan Ray Tanner. My **nickname** is Dart.

❶ Hi, I'm Liz. Liz Kim. My **first name** is Elizabeth, but **everyone calls me** Liz.

Mrs. _Maria_   _Sanchez_
FIRST   MIDDLE   LAST
☐ single ☑ married

Mr. _Don_   _Ray Tanner_
FIRST   MIDDLE   LAST
☑ single ☐ married

Ms. ___ _—_ _Kim_
FIRST   MIDDLE   LAST
☑ single ☐ married

Miss, Mrs., Ms., Mr.?

Liz Kim is single.	▶ **Ms.** Kim or **Miss** Kim
Ana Sanchez is married.	▶ **Ms.** Sanchez or **Mrs.** Sanchez
Don Tanner is single.	▶ **Mr.** Tanner
Ana's husband is married.	▶ **Mr.** Sanchez

About you **B** Complete the sentences. Then compare with a partner.

1. My first name is _____ .
2. Everyone calls me _____ .
3. My last name is _____ .
4. My middle name is _____ .
5. My nickname is _____ .
6. My teacher's name is _____ .

C 🔊 1.06 Listen and say the alphabet. Circle all the letters in your name.

Aa	Bb	Cc	Dd	Ee	Ff	Gg	Hh	Ii	Jj	Kk	Ll	Mm
Nn	Oo	Pp	Qq	Rr	Ss	Tt	Uu	Vv	Ww	Xx	Yy	Zz

D 🔊 1.07 Listen. How do you spell Catherine's last name? Then practice the conversation with a partner. Use your own names.

A What's your name?
B Catherine Ravelli.
A How do you spell *Catherine*?
B C-A-T-H-E-R-I-N-E.
A Thanks. And your last name?
B R-A-V-E-L-L-I.

About you **E** **Class activity** Ask your classmates their names. Make a list.

4

2 Building language

A 🔊 1.08 Listen. Which classroom is Carmen in this year? What about Jenny? Practice the conversation.

Mr. Martin   Good morning. Are you here for an English class?
Carmen   Yes, I am. I'm Carmen Rivera.
Mr. Martin   OK. You're in Room B.
Jenny   And I'm Jenny.
Mr. Martin   Are you Jenny Loo?
Jenny   No, I'm not. I'm Jenny Lim. Am I in Room B, too?
Mr. Martin   Yes. . . . Wait – no, you're not. You're in Room G.
Jenny   Oh, no! Carmen, we're not in the same class!

Class Registration
- Music
- English
- French

Figure it out

B Can you complete the conversations? Use the conversation above to help you.

1. A ___Are___ you Jenny Loo?
   B No, I _____ not. I _____ Lucy.

2. A _____ you here for an English class?
   B Yes, I _____ . I _____ Carmen Rivera.

3. A _____ I in your class?
   B Yes. _____ in my class.

3 Grammar   The verb *be*: *I, you,* and *we* 🔊 1.09

Extra practice p. 139

Statements

		Contractions
I'm Jenny.	**I'm not** Carmen.	*I'm = I am*
You're in Room G.	**You're not** in Room B.	*you're = you are*
We're in different classes.	**We're not** in the same class.	*we're = we are*

Questions and short answers

Are you Jenny?   **Am I** in Room B?   **Are we** in the same class?
Yes, **I am**.   Yes, **you are**.   Yes, **we are**.
No, **I'm not**.   No, **you're not**.   No, **we're not**.

✗ Common errors

Use the full form of the verb *be* in short answers with *yes*.

Yes, I am. (NOT Yes, ~~I'm~~.)
Yes, we are. (NOT Yes, ~~we're~~.)

A Complete the conversations. Then practice with a partner.

1. A ___Are___ you Chris?
   B Yes, I _____ . _____ we in the same class?
   A Yes, we _____ . I _____ Dino.
   B Hi, Dino. Nice to meet you.

2. A Hey, Amy. _____ you here for an English class?
   B No, I _____ not. I _____ here for a French class.
   A OK. See you later.

(((Sounds right p. 137

About you

B Pair work Choose a conversation and practice it. Use your own information.

Lesson C / Personal information

1 Numbers 0–10

A 🔊 1.10 Listen and say the numbers.

0	1	2	3	4	5	6	7	8	9	10
zero	one	two	three	four	five	six	seven	eight	nine	ten

B 🔊 1.11 Listen. Then practice.

❶ My passport number is 649-321-508.

❷ My ID number is 259-62-1883.

❸ My cell phone number is 216-555-7708. My email address is dsmith6@cup.org.

PASSPORT / PASSEPORT CANADA
Passport No./No de passeport 649 321 508
Surname/Nom BARTON
Given names/Prénoms JAMES DAVID
Nationality/Nationalité CANADIAN / CANADIEN
P<CAN<BARTON<<JAMESDAVID<<<<<<<<<<<<<<<
<<<<<<<649321508<<<<<<<<<<<<<<<<<<<<

GRLEN STATE UNIVERSITY
GSU
ELLEN M. JONES   ID: 259-62-1883

California Union of Pilots
Daniel Smith
TELEPHONE: 216-555-7708
EMAIL: dsmith6@cup.org

> **ℹ️ Note**
>
> **Numbers and email addresses**
>
> 216-555-7708 = "two-one-six, five-five-five, seven-seven-**oh (zero)**-eight"
> dsmith6@cup.org = "d-smith-six-**at**-c-u-p-**dot**-org"

2 Building language

A 🔊 1.12 Listen. What is Victor's phone number? Practice the conversation.

Receptionist Hi! Are you a member?
Victor No, I'm just here for the day.
Receptionist OK. So, what's your name, please?
Victor Victor Lopez.
Receptionist And what's your phone number?
Victor It's 646-555-3048.
Receptionist And your email address?
Victor Um . . . it's vlopez6@cup.org.
Receptionist OK. So it's $10 for today. Here's your pass.
Victor Thanks.

Figure it out

B Can you complete these questions and answers? Use the conversation above to help you. Then practice with a partner.

1. A What's your name?
   B _____ Joe Garrett.

2. A What's your _____ _____?
   B It's 646-555-4628.

3. A What's _____ _____?
   B _____ joe.garrett@cup.org.

3 Grammar *What's . . . ?; It's . . .* ◀)) 1.13

Extra practice p. 139

What's your name?   **My name's** Victor Lopez.
What's your email address?   **It's** vlopez6@cup.org.
What's your phone number?   **It's** 646-555-3048.

What's = What is   *name's = name is*   *It's = It is*

A Write a question for each answer. Compare with a partner. Then practice.

1. A *What's your first name* ?
   B My first name's Haley – H-A-L-E-Y.

2. A _____ ?
   B My last name? Osman – O-S-M-A-N.

3. A _____ ?
   B 347-555-2801.

4. A _____ ?
   B It's j.song6@cup.org.

5. A _____ ?
   B My teacher's name? It's Ms. Rossi.

6. A _____ ?
   B My student ID number? Wait – it's 36-88-972.

About you **B** Pair work Ask and answer the questions. Give your own answers.

A *What's your first name?*
B *It's Silvia – S-I-L-V-I-A.*

✗ Common errors

Don't start an answer with *Is.*

What's your name?
It's Silvia. (NOT Is Silvia.)

4 Listening and speaking Memberships

A ◀)) 1.14 Listen to the conversations. Complete the membership cards.

1.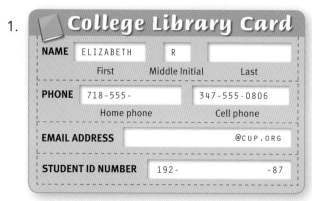

2.

About you **B** Pair work Now complete this form for a partner. Ask questions.

TOUCHSTONE CONVERSATION CLUB Membership application

FIRST NAME	MIDDLE INITIAL	LAST NAME

CELL PHONE	EMAIL ADDRESS	STUDENT ID NUMBER

A *What's your first name?*
B *Rashid.*
A *How do you spell that?*

1 Conversation strategy *How about you?*

A Look at the photo. Adam and Alicia are strangers. Guess three things they say.

B 🔊 1.15 Listen. Who's on vacation? Who's a student? Who's here for the concert?

Alicia	Hi. How are you doing?
Adam	Pretty good. How about you?
Alicia	Good, thanks. It's a beautiful day.
Adam	Yeah, it is. Are you here for the concert?
Alicia	Yes. How about you?
Adam	Well, yeah, but I'm a student here, too. So are you on vacation?
Alicia	Yes, I am. By the way, I'm Alicia.
Adam	I'm Adam. Nice to meet you. Well, have a nice day.
Alicia	Thanks. You too.

C Notice how Adam and Alicia say *How about you?* to ask the same questions.

"How are you doing?"
"Pretty good. How about you?"

D Complete the conversations. Then practice with a partner.

1. A Hello. Are you here for the festival?

   B Yeah, I am. _____ ?

   A Yeah. Me too.

2. A Hi. How are you doing?

   B Good, thanks. How about you?

   A _____ .

3. A Are you a student?

   B No, I'm a teacher.

   _____ ?

   A I'm a teacher, too.

4. A It's a beautiful day. Are you on vacation?

   B Yes, I am. _____ ?

   A No. I'm a student here.

5. A I'm here on business. How about you?

   B No. _____ .

   A Nice. Well, have a great vacation.

2 Strategy plus Everyday expressions

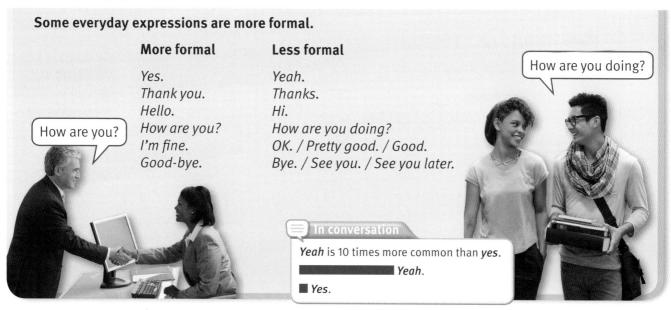

Some everyday expressions are more formal.

More formal	Less formal
Yes.	Yeah.
Thank you.	Thanks.
Hello.	Hi.
How are you?	How are you doing?
I'm fine.	OK. / Pretty good. / Good.
Good-bye.	Bye. / See you. / See you later.

> How are you doing?

> How are you?

In conversation

Yeah is 10 times more common than *yes*.

▬▬▬▬▬▬▬▬▬ *Yeah*.
▬ *Yes*.

About you Complete these conversations with expressions from the box above. Then practice with a partner.

1. Formal conversation

Jeff   _____Hello_____ , Mrs. Swan. _____ ?

Mrs. Swan   _____ , thank you. Uh, Jeff, are you here for English 3?

Jeff   _____ , I am.

Mrs. Swan   Then you're in Room B. I'm the teacher for English 2.

Jeff   Oh, _____ . Well, have a nice day.

Mrs. Swan   _____ . You too. Enjoy your class! _____ .

2. Less formal conversation

Kathy   Hi, Mike, _____ ?

Mike   _____ . How about you?

Kathy   _____ . Are you here for a class?

Mike   _____ , I am. I'm here for yoga. How about you?

Kathy   Oh, I'm here for a music class.

Mike   Nice. Well, enjoy your class!

Kathy   _____ . You too.

Mike   OK. _____ .

3 Strategies In the park

About you **Pair work** Look at the picture. Choose an activity in the park. Role-play a conversation.

A *Hi, how are you?*

B *Good, thanks. How about you?*

A *Pretty good. Are you here for the movie?*

Free talk p. 129

TODAY IN THE PARK

Yoga
Concert
Movie

PARK

Learning tip *Learning expressions*

Write new expressions with their responses, like this:

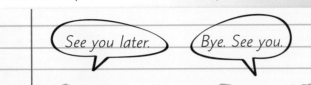

See you later.   Bye. See you.

Write a response for each expression.

1. Hello.

2. Good morning.

3. Hi, I'm Helen.

4. How are you?

5. Have a nice day.

6. See you tomorrow.

7. Have a good evening.

8. Good night.

On your own

Before your next class, say *hello* and *good-bye* (in English!) to three people.

Hi. How are you?

✓ Can Do! Now I can . . .

| ✓ I can . . . | ? I need to review how to . . . |

- [ ] say *hello* and *good-bye*.
- [ ] introduce myself.
- [ ] ask for, give, and spell names.
- [ ] ask and answer questions about names, phone numbers, and email addresses.
- [ ] complete an application form.
- [ ] use *How about you?* to ask the same question.
- [ ] use formal and informal everyday expressions like *Thanks* and *Thank you*.
- [ ] understand conversations about personal information.

In class

✓ Can Do! In this unit, you learn how to . . .

Lesson A
- Ask and say where people are
- Use *be* with *he, she,* and *they*

Lesson B
- Talk about things you take to class using *a / an*
- Ask about things using *this* and *these*

Lesson C
- Ask where things are in a classroom
- Say who owns things using possessive *'s* and *s'*

Lesson D
- Ask for help in class
- Respond to *I'm sorry* and *Thanks*

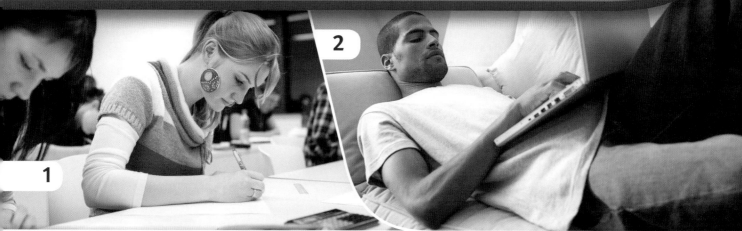

Before you begin . . .

Where are these people? Match the pictures with the sentences.

☐ He's at home. ☐ *1* They're in class. ☐ She's at work.

☐ They're at the library. ☐ She's at the gym.

Miss Nelson	Where's Hiroki? Is he here today?
Alison	No, he's not. Maybe he's at work.
Miss Nelson	OK. How about Ellen?
Alison	I don't know. I think she's sick.
Miss Nelson	Oh. OK. Are Carmen and Suzanna here?
Alison	No, they're in the cafeteria.
Miss Nelson	They're late again. OK. And Nick?
Alison	He's over there. I think he's asleep!

The verb BE

Nick

Alison

Jun

Hiroki

Ellen

Carmen and Suzanna

1 Getting started

A Look at the pictures. Who is in class? Who is absent?

B ◀)) 1.16 Listen. Who is sick today? Who is late? Who is asleep? Practice the conversation.

Figure it out **C** Circle the correct words. Use the conversation above to help you.

1. A Hiroki? Is he here today?

   B No, **he's / she's** at work.

2. A Ellen? **Is / Are** she in class?

   B No, **she is / she's not**. She's sick.

3. A **Is / Are** Carmen and Suzanna late?

   B Yes. **They're / She's** in the cafeteria.

4. A **Is / Are** Nick here?

   B Yes, **he's / he** here. I think **he's / is** asleep.

2 Grammar The verb *be*: *he*, *she*, and *they* ◀))) 1.17

Extra practice p. 140

Hiroki**'s** at work. **He's** at work.	Hiroki**'s not** here. **He's not** here.	**Is** Hiroki at work? Yes, **he is.** **Is he** here? No, **he's not.**
Ellen**'s** sick. **She's** sick.	Ellen**'s not** in class. **She's not** in class.	**Is** Ellen sick? Yes, **she is.** **Is she** in class? No, **she's not.**
Carmen and Suzanna **are** late. **They're** late.	Carmen and Suzanna **are not** here. **They're not** here.	**Are they** late? Yes, **they are.** **Are they** here? No, **they're not.**

Hiroki's = Hiroki is   He's = He is   They're = They are
Ellen's = Ellen is   She's = She is

In conversation

People usually shorten *is* to *'s* after names.

Hiroki's at work. Ellen's not in class.

A These students are also in Miss Nelson's class. Where are they today? Complete the sentences.

1. Daniel 's_____ at the gym.
    He _____ in class.
    He _____ sick.

2. Liz and Tom _____ in class.
    They _____ in the cafeteria.
    They _____ at the library.
    Tom _____ asleep.

3. Della _____ in class.
    She _____ absent.
    Fred _____ in class, too.
    He _____ sick.

B Complete the questions about the students above. Write true answers. Then ask and answer the questions with a partner.

1. ____*Is*____ Daniel sick?
2. _____ Liz in class?
3. _____ Liz and Tom at the gym?

4. _____ Tom asleep?
5. _____ Della and Fred in class?
6. _____ Della sick?

*A **Is Daniel sick?***

*B **No, he's not. He's at the gym.***

3 Listening Who's absent today?

A ◀))) 1.18 Listen. It's the next day. Are these students in class or absent? Check (✓) the boxes.
Then listen again and match the two parts of the sentence.

	In class	Absent
1. Ellen		
2. Carmen		
3. Hiroki		
4. Alison		

1. Ellen's _____   a. sick.
2. Carmen's _____   b. asleep.
3. Hiroki's _____   c. at work.
4. Alison's _____   d. at the library.

About you **B** **Pair work** Ask and answer questions about your classmates.

*A **Is Samir absent today?***

*B **No, he's not. He's in class. He's over there.***

1 Building vocabulary

A 🔊 1.19 Here are some things students take to class. Write *a* or *an* before each item. Then listen and say the words. Check your answers.

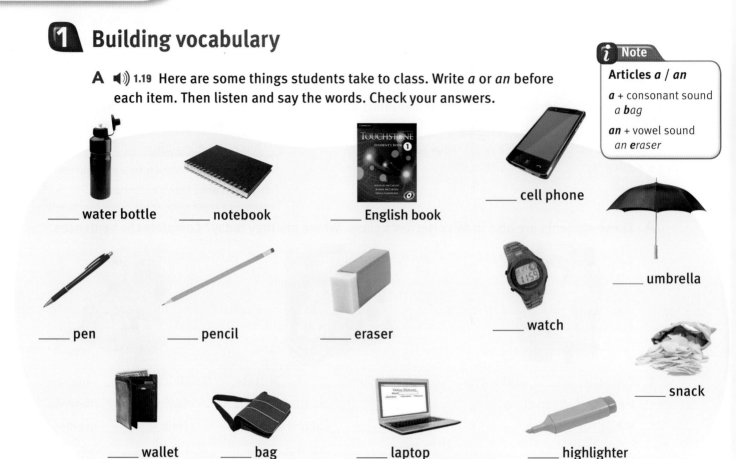

_____ water bottle   _____ notebook   _____ English book   _____ cell phone

_____ umbrella

_____ pen   _____ pencil   _____ eraser   _____ watch

_____ snack

_____ wallet   _____ bag   _____ laptop   _____ highlighter
                _____ online dictionary

Word sort **B** Make two lists of things *you* take to class. Use *a* and *an*. Compare with a partner.

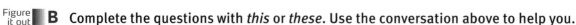

a	*an*
a pencil	*an umbrella*

2 Building language

A 🔊 1.20 Listen. Which things are Laura's?
Then practice the conversation.

Alan   What's this? Laura, is this your cell phone?
Laura Yes, it is. Thanks. Oh, and these are my headphones.
Alan   They're cool. OK. See you tomorrow. Wait. Is this your bag?
Laura Yeah.
Alan   And are these your keys?
Laura Yeah, they are. Wait – my sunglasses?
Alan   They're on your head!

Figure it out **B** Complete the questions with *this* or *these*. Use the conversation above to help you.

1. Is _____ your new computer?   2. Are _____ your keys?

3 Grammar   *This* and *these*; noun plurals ◀)) 1.21

Extra practice p. 140

This is a cell phone.

What's this?
   It's a cell phone.

Is this your cell phone?
   Yes, **it is.**
   No, **it's not.**

These are headphones.

What are these?
   They're headphones.

Are these your headphones?
   Yes, **they are.**
   No, **they're not.**

Regular plurals
bag	bag**s**
watch	watch**es**
dictionary	dictiona**ries**
key	key**s**

Irregular plurals
man	m**e**n
woman	wom**e**n
child	child**ren**

Some nouns are only plural:
glasses, sunglasses, scissors, jeans

Complete the questions and answers about the pictures. Then practice with a partner.

1.

A __*Is*__ this your _____ ?
B Yes, _____ . Thank you.

2.

A What's _____ ?
B _____ a computer bag.

3.

A _____ these your _____ ?
B Yes, _____ . Thanks.

4.

A Are _____ your _____ ?
B No, _____ .

5.

A Is _____ an eraser?
B Yes, _____ .

6.

A What are _____ ?
B I think _____ pens.

4 Speaking naturally   Noun plural endings

/s/ wallet**s**, book**s**	/z/ pen**s**, key**s**	/ɪz/ watch**es**, orang**es**

A ◀)) 1.22 Listen and repeat the words above. Notice which nouns add a syllable in the plural.

B ◀)) 1.23 Listen. Do the nouns end in /s/ or /z/, or do they add the syllable /ɪz/?
Check (✓) the correct column.

What's in your bag?	/s/-/z/	/ɪz/
1. my sunglasses	☐	✓
2. three notebooks	☐	☐
3. two brushes	☐	☐
4. five credit cards	☐	☐
5. two sandwiches	☐	☐

About you **C Class activity** Ask classmates, "What's in your bag?" Who has
something unusual?

   A *What's in your bag, Carlos?*
   B *A wallet, two oranges . . .*

✗ Common errors

Don't forget *a / an*, *my*, *your*,
etc. before a singular noun.

*It's **an** eraser.* (NOT ~~It's eraser.~~)

1 Building vocabulary

A 🔊 1.24 Listen and say the words. Which things are in your classroom? Check (✓) the boxes. What else is in your classroom?

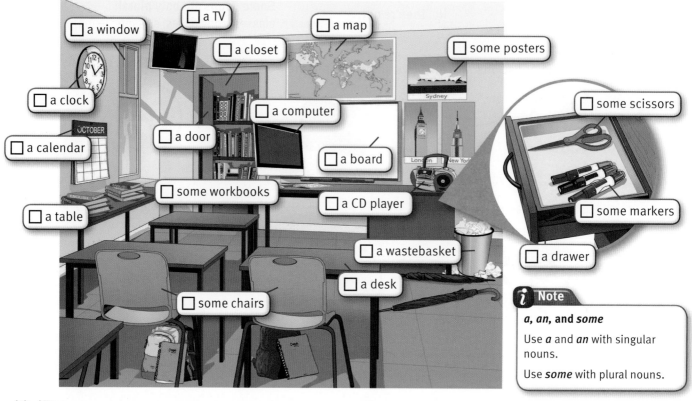

☐ a window
☐ a TV
☐ a map
☐ some posters
☐ a closet
☐ a clock
☐ a computer
☐ some scissors
☐ a calendar
☐ a door
☐ a board
☐ some workbooks
☐ a CD player
☐ some markers
☐ a table
☐ a wastebasket
☐ a drawer
☐ a desk
☐ some chairs

> **i Note**
>
> **a, an, and some**
>
> Use **a** and **an** with singular nouns.
>
> Use **some** with plural nouns.

Word sort **B** Look at the pictures. What things are in these places in the classroom above? Complete the chart.

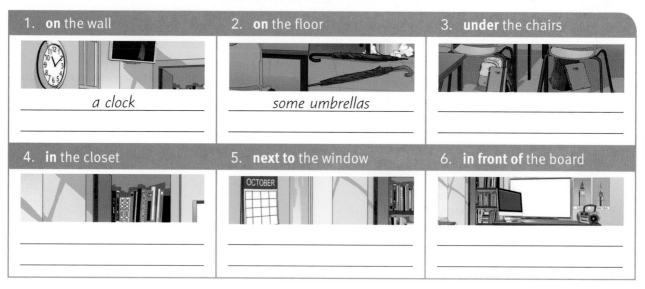

1. **on** the wall	2. **on** the floor	3. **under** the chairs
a clock	*some umbrellas*	
4. **in** the closet	5. **next to** the window	6. **in front of** the board

About you **C** Pair work Ask and answer questions about your classroom.

A *What's on the wall?*

B *A board, some posters . . .*

Vocabulary notebook p. 20

2 Building language

A 🔊 **1.25** Listen. What is the teacher looking for?
Practice the conversation.

Mr. Kern Hello, I'm Mr. Kern.
Paula Hi. I'm Paula. Uh, where's Ms. Moore?
Mr. Kern She's sick today.
Paula Oh, no! So is the grammar test today?
Mr. Kern Yes, it is. . . . OK, so, this is the teacher's book,
but where are the students' test papers?
Paula Uh, they're in Ms. Moore's desk.
Mr. Kern Oh, it's locked. Now, where's the key?
Paula I don't know. Sorry.
Mr. Kern Oh. Well, no test today then. Oh wait.
It's right here in my coat pocket.

Figure it out

B Circle the correct words. Use the conversation above to help you.
Then ask and answer the questions with a partner.

1. **Where's** / **Where** the key?
2. **Where are** / **Where's** the students' test papers?
3. What's in the **teacher's** / **teachers'** desk?
4. What's in **Mr. Kern** / **Mr. Kern's** pocket?

3 Grammar Questions with *Where*; possessive *'s* and *s'* 🔊 **1.26**   **Extra practice p. 140**

Questions with *Where*	Possessives	*a / an* vs. *the*

Where's the key?
  I don't know.
	Add *'s* **to names.**
	  Ms. Moore**'s** desk
		It's in **a** desk.
		(I don't know which desk.)

Where are the students' tests?
  They're in the desk.
	Add *'s* **to singular nouns.**
	  the teacher**'s** book / books
		It's in **the** desk.
		(We know which desk.)

Where's = Where is	**Add** *'* **to plural nouns.** the student**s'** books	

A **Pair work** Circle *is* or *are* and correct the possessives. Then ask and answer the questions
about the classroom in the picture above. Can you ask four more questions?

1. Where **'s** / **are** the teacher's desk?
2. Where **'s** / **are** the students test books?
3. Where **'s** / **are** Ms. Moores key?
4. Where **'s** / **are** Mr. Kerns coat?
5. Where **'s** / **are** the teachers computer?
6. Where **'s** / **are** the students workbooks?

A *Where's the teacher's desk?*
B *It's in front of the board.*

About you

B Write four questions with *Where . . . ?* about things in your classroom. Use these ideas or add
your own. Then ask a partner your questions.

the teacher's bag   the students' bags

the teacher's computer   the students' homework papers

Sounds right p. 137

17

1 Conversation strategy Asking for help in class

A Can you match the questions and answers?

1. How do you spell *eraser*? _____
2. Can I borrow your pencil? _____
3. What's the word for this in English? _____

a. Sure.
b. Watch.
c. E-R-A-S-E-R.

B 🔊 1.27 Listen. How many times does Ming-wei ask for help?

Ming-wei	Excuse me, what's the word for this in English?
Sonia	*Highlighter*.
Ming-wei	Thanks.
Sonia	Sure.
Ming-wei	Uh . . . how do you spell it?
Sonia	I don't know. Sorry.
Ming-wei	That's OK. Thanks anyway. . . . Can I borrow a pen, please?
Sonia	Sure. Here you go.
Ming-wei	Thank you.
Sonia	You're welcome.
Ms. Larsen	OK. Open your books to page 4.
Ming-wei	Excuse me, can you repeat that, please? What page?
Ms. Larsen	Sure. Page 4.

C Notice how Ming-wei asks for help in class. Find his questions.

"What's the word for this in English?"

"How do you spell it?"

D Complete the conversations with questions from the box. Then practice with a partner.

Can you repeat that, please?   What's the word for this in English?
Can I borrow an eraser, please?   How do you spell *highlighter*?

1. A *How do you spell highlighter* ?

   B H-I-G-H-L-I-G-H-T-E-R, I think.

2. A OK. Open your workbooks.

   B _____ ?

   A Yes. Open your workbooks.

3. A _____ ?

   B Sure. Here you go.

4. A _____ ?

   B I don't know. Maybe it's *wastebasket*.

About you ▌ **E Pair work** Practice the conversations again. Use your own ideas.

18

2 Strategy plus Common expressions and responses

Here are some responses to *Thank you* and *I'm sorry*:

When people say . . .	You can say . . .
Thank you.	*You're welcome.*
Thanks.	*Sure.*
I'm sorry.	*That's OK.*
I'm sorry. I don't know.	*That's OK. Thanks anyway.*

That's OK.

I'm sorry.

🔊 **1.28** Circle the correct response. Listen and check your answers. Then practice with a partner.

1. A Here's your pencil.
    B Thank you.
    A I'm sorry. / (You're welcome.)

2. A Here's a sandwich for you.
    B Thanks!
    A **Sure. / Thanks anyway.**

3. A Can I borrow a pen, please?
    B I'm sorry. This is my only pen.
    A Oh, OK. **Thanks anyway. / You're welcome.**

4. A I'm sorry I'm late.
    B **Sure. / That's OK.**

3 Listening and strategies Following instructions

A 🔊 **1.29** Match the pictures with the instructions. Then listen to the class and check your answers.

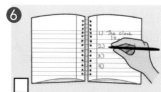

a. Close your books.
b. Listen to the conversation.
c. Look at the picture.
d. Open your books, and turn to page 9.
e. Read the questions aloud.
f. Answer the questions. Write the answers in your notebook.

B 🔊 **1.29** Listen again. Complete the questions the students ask.

1. I'm sorry. What page are we on? Page _____ ?
2. What's the word for this? Is it _____ ?
3. Can you _____ that, please?
4. How do you spell _____ ?
5. Excuse me. What's a _____ ?
6. Can I borrow a _____ , please?

C Class activity Ask five classmates for help. Use the questions in this lesson.

A *Can I borrow your eraser, please?*
B *Sure.*
A *Thanks.*
B *You're welcome.*

Free talk p. 129

Vocabulary notebook / My things

Learning tip *Linking things with places*
Make lists of things you keep in different places.

in my bag - my wallet, a pen, some books

1 Label the things on a student's desk.

some books

2 Now make lists of your things.

What's in your bag?	What's in your wallet?	What's under your desk?	What's in your pockets?

On your own
Find a magazine with pictures of things. Label the pictures. How many words can you label?

Now I can . . .

✓ I can . . .   ? I need to review how to . . .

- ask and say where people are.
- ask and say where things are in a classroom.
- talk about things I take to class.
- talk about classroom objects.
- say who owns things.
- ask for help in class.
- respond when people say *Thanks* and *I'm sorry*.
- understand conversations about where people are.
- follow classroom instructions.

20

Favorite people

✓ Can Do! In this unit, you learn how to . . .

Lesson A
- Talk about celebrities using *my*, *your*, *his*, *her*, *our*, and *their*

Lesson B
- Describe people's personalities
- Ask and answer *yes-no* questions

Lesson C
- Say the ages of your family members
- Ask information questions about family members

Lesson D
- Show interest in a conversation
- Say *Really?* to show interest or surprise

Before you begin . . .

Match each sentence with a picture. For each sentence, think of people you know.

| ☐ He's an artist. | ☐ He's a singer. | ☐ She's a writer. |
| *1* She's an actor. | ☐ They're tennis players. | ☐ They're soccer players. |

①

Zach   Who's that?

Haley   It's Johnny Depp. He's my favorite actor. He's so good-looking! His new movie's great.

Zach   Hmm . . . what else is on?

②

Haley   There's a concert. Oh, it's Adele! I love her new album. Her voice is amazing.

Zach   Adele?

Haley   Yeah. She's a famous singer.

Zach   Oh. Um, how about some sports?

③

Haley   Look. They're my favorite tennis players. Their matches are always exciting. You're a tennis fan, right?

Zach   Um, not really. Where's the remote?

Haley   Here you go.

④

Zach   Great – a football game. And it's our favorite team.

Haley   You mean *your* favorite team. You know I'm not a football fan.

1 Getting started

A   Look at the pictures. Haley and Zach are watching TV. What's on TV today?

B   🔊 1.30 Listen. Is Haley a sports fan? How about Zach?

Figure it out

C   Can you complete the sentences? Use the conversation above to help you.

1. Johnny Depp is an actor. _____ movies are really exciting.

2. Adele is a famous singer. _____ new album is very good.

3. They're tennis players. _____ matches are always great.

4. My best friend and I are soccer fans. _____ favorite team is not very good.

22

2 Grammar *Be* in statements; possessive adjectives 🔊 1.31

Extra practice p. 141

I'm	a Johnny Depp fan.	**My**	favorite actor is Johnny Depp.
You're	a tennis fan.	**Your**	favorite sport is tennis.
He's	an actor.	**His**	new movie is great.
She's	a famous singer.	**Her**	voice is amazing.
We're	Giants fans.	**Our**	favorite team is the Giants.
They're	tennis players.	**Their**	matches are exciting.

> ✖ **Common errors**
>
> Don't add "**s**" to a possessive adjective.
>
> *Their* matches are exciting.
> (NOT ~~*Theirs matches*~~ are exciting.)

A Complete the conversations with expressions from the box. Use capital letters when necessary. Compare with a partner. Then practice.

he's	his	✓my	she's	they're	you're
her	I'm	our	their	we're	your

1. A ___*My*___ favorite band is Foo Fighters.
   _____ a big fan of _____ music.

   B Yeah. _____ good.

2. A In my family, _____ big soccer fans.
   It's _____ favorite sport.

   B Yeah? My brother is a soccer fan. _____ a Manchester United fan.

3. A What's _____ favorite movie?

   B *The Hunger Games*.

   A Oh, yeah. Josh Hutcherson is one of my favorite actors. _____ movies are always good.

4. A _____ a big fan of Adele, right?

   B Yeah, _____ voice is amazing. _____ very talented.

About you **B** **Pair work** Are any of the statements above true for you? Tell a partner.

3 Talk about it My favorite . . .

Write the names of your favorite celebrities below. Then talk about them with a partner. How many things can you say?

actor	*Andrew Garfield*	**sports team**	
singer		**writer**	
band		**artist**	

"My favorite actor is Andrew Garfield. His movies are good."

23

1 Building vocabulary

A 🔊 1.32 Look at Jason's sketches on his blog and read his comments. Then listen and say the sentences. Do you know people like these? Tell the class.

This is Jenn, a friend from high school. She's very **interesting**. She's in a band!

This is me with my best friend, Ethan. He's **lazy**.

This is my neighbor and his son. My neighbor is **friendly** and **outgoing**, but his son is **quiet** and **shy**.

My math teacher's very **smart**. And she's really **nice**, too. She's always **fun** in class.

Word sort **B** How many words can you think of to describe people you know? Complete the chart. Then tell a partner.

My best friend	My classmates	My neighbors	My _____
very smart			

"My best friend is very smart. He's a good student."

📓 Vocabulary notebook p. 30

2 Building language

A 🔊 1.33 Listen. What is Tim's new boss like? Practice the conversation.

Dana So how's your new job? Are you busy?

Tim Yes. It's hard work, you know. I'm tired.

Dana Really? What are your co-workers like? Are they nice?

Tim Yes, they are. They're really friendly.

Dana Great. And is your boss OK?

Tim She is, yeah. She's nice. Um . . . she's not very strict.

Dana Good, because you're late for work.

Figure it out **B** Can you complete these questions and answers? Then ask and answer the questions with a partner. Use your own information.

1. A What's your teacher like? _____ fun?

   B Yes, she _____ .

2. A What are your classmates like? _____ they friendly?

   B Yes, they _____ .

3. A _____ your English class hard?

   B No, it's not.

3 Grammar *Yes-no* questions and answers; negatives ◀)) 1.34

Extra practice p. 141

Am I late?	Yes, **you are.**	No, **you're not.**	**You're not** late.
Are you busy?	Yes, **I am.**	No, **I'm not.**	**I'm not** busy.
Is he tired?	Yes, **he is.**	No, **he's not.**	**He's not** tired.
Is she strict?	Yes, **she is.**	No, **she's not.**	**She's not** strict. (My boss **isn't** strict.)
Is it hard work?	Yes, **it is.**	No, **it's not.**	**It's not** hard work.
Are we late?	Yes, **we are.**	No, **we're not.**	**We're not** late.
Are they nice?	Yes, **they are.**	No, **they're not.**	**They're not** nice. (My co-workers **aren't** nice.)

A Complete the conversations. Compare with a partner. Then practice.

> **In conversation**
>
> People use *'s not* and *'re not* after pronouns.
>
> > She*'s not* strict.
> > They*'re not* nice.
>
> *Isn't* and *aren't* often follow nouns.
>
> > My boss *isn't* strict.
> > My co-workers *aren't* nice.

1. A How's school? ___*Are*___ your classes interesting?

   B Yes, _____ . My teachers are very smart.

2. A _____ your English class easy?

   B No, _____ . The lessons _____ easy.

3. A _____ you outgoing in class?

   B Yes, _____ . I _____ always outgoing.

4. A _____ your English teacher strict?

   B No, he _____ .

5. A What's your job like? _____ it fun?

   B Yes, _____ . My boss _____ very strict.

6. A What are your neighbors like? _____ they nice?

   B No, _____ . They _____ very friendly.

About you **B** Pair work Ask and answer the questions. Give your own information.

4 Speaking naturally *Is he . . . ?* or *Is she . . . ?*

"izee"
Is he *a student?*

"ishee"
Is she *a student?*

A ◀)) 1.35 Listen and repeat the questions above. Notice the pronunciation of *Is he . . . ?* and *Is she . . . ?*

B ◀)) 1.36 Listen. Do you hear *Is he . . . ?* or *Is she . . . ?* Circle *he* or *she*.

1. Is **he** / (**she**) a friend from high school?
2. Is **he** / **she** a college student?
3. Is **he** / **she** shy?

4. Is **he** / **she** smart?
5. Is **he** / **she** interesting?
6. Is **he** / **she** fun?

About you **C** Pair work Find out about your partner's best friend. Ask and answer questions like the ones above.

A *So your best friend. Is he a friend from high school?*
B *No, he's a neighbor.*

1 Building vocabulary

A 🔊 1.37 Look at Erica Rivera's family tree. Who are her parents? Who are her grandparents? Listen and say the words.

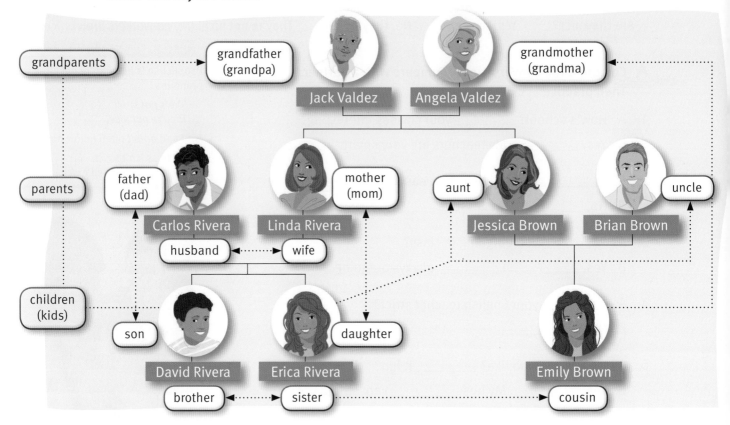

B How are these people related to Erica Rivera? Complete the chart. Compare with a partner.

Carlos Rivera	*father*	Jack Valdez		Emily Brown	
Linda Rivera		Angela Valdez		Brian Brown	
David Rivera		Jessica Brown			

"Who's Carlos Rivera?"   "He's Erica's father."

Vocabulary notebook p. 30

C 🔊 1.38 Listen and say the numbers.

10	ten	16	sixteen	22	twenty-two	28	twenty-eight	70	seventy
11	eleven	17	seventeen	23	twenty-three	29	twenty-nine	80	eighty
12	twelve	18	eighteen	24	twenty-four	30	thirty	90	ninety
13	thirteen	19	nineteen	25	twenty-five	40	forty	100	one hundred
14	fourteen	20	twenty	26	twenty-six	50	fifty	101	a hundred and one
15	fifteen	21	twenty-one	27	twenty-seven	60	sixty		

D Pair work Student A: Tell your partner the names and ages of your family members.
Student B: Write the information you hear. Then check the information with your partner.

A *My mother's name is Sandra.*
   She's fifty-five.

Eva's mother –
Sandra, 55

B *Is your mother's name Sandra?*
A **Yes, it is.**

2 Building language

A 🔊 **1.39** Listen. How old are Erica's grandparents?
Practice the conversation.

Padma So who's this?

Erica My grandma. And this is my grandpa.
He's a nice man. He's seventy-eight now.

Padma Really? And how old is your grandmother?

Erica She's seventy-two.

Padma She's very pretty. What's her name?

Erica Angela.

Padma That's a nice name. So where are
your grandparents from originally?

Erica They're from Texas.

Figure it out **B** Can you complete these questions?
Then ask and answer the questions with a partner.

1. __*Who's*__ the man in the photo?

2. _____ his wife's name?

3. _____ Erica's grandparents? 70? 75?

4. _____ they from originally?

3 Grammar Information questions with *be* 🔊 1.40

Extra practice p. 141

you	**he / she / it**	**they**
How are you? I'm fine.	**Who's this?** It's my grandmother.	**How are your parents?** They're fine, thanks.
Where are you from? I'm from Florida.	**Where's she from?** She's from Texas.	**Where are they today?** They're at home.
How old are you? I'm twenty-three.	**What's she like?** She's very smart.	**What are their names?** Their names are Linda and Carlos.

A Unscramble the questions. Compare with a partner. Then ask and answer the questions.

1. your / are / parents / how / ?   *How are your parents?*

2. parents' / what / names / your / are / ? _____

3. your / is / old / how / father / ?   _____

4. like / what's / mother / your / ?   _____

5. today / your / where's / mother / ?   _____

6. are / from / grandparents / your / where / ? _____

7. your / aunt / who's / favorite / ?   _____

About you **B** Write four more questions to ask your partner about his or her family. Then ask and answer
the questions.

A **What's your father like?**
B **He's very outgoing.**

🔊 **Sounds right** p. 137

A songwriter? Really?

1 Conversation strategy Showing interest

A Are any of your friends artists, singers, or songwriters? Are any of your friends from another country? Tell the class.

B 🔊 1.41 Listen. What do you find out about Lucy's friend?

Hugo	What's that?
Lucy	It's a painting. I know the artist. She's a friend of mine.
Hugo	Really? It's great. What's her name?
Lucy	Carla. I think her work is amazing.
Hugo	Yeah. Where's she from?
Lucy	Paris originally.
Hugo	Paris? Wow. Is she a professional artist?
Lucy	Yeah. And she's a singer – songwriter.
Hugo	A songwriter? Really? What are her songs like?
Lucy	Here. Listen.
Hugo	Hmm. Interesting. Well, her *paintings* are good.

C Notice how Hugo shows interest. He repeats words and asks questions. Find examples in the conversation.

"She's from Paris originally."
"Paris? Wow. Is she a professional artist?"

D Complete the responses. Then practice with a partner.

1. A My friend Rumiko is a singer.

   B *A singer*_____? Is she in a band?

2. A My best friend's name is Dmitry.

   B _____? Where's he from?

3. A My brother is a writer.

   B _____? Is he famous?

4. A My cousins are big baseball fans.

   B _____? What's their favorite team?

About you **E** **Pair work** Practice the conversations above again with your own information. Show interest by repeating words and asking questions. Can you continue the conversations?

A My friend Mindy is a student.
B A student? Is she a student here?

2 Strategy plus *Really?*

People say *Really?* to show they are interested or surprised.

She's a friend of mine.

Really?

In conversation

Really is one of the top 50 words.

A Pair work Complete the conversations with the correct responses from the box. Then practice with a partner.

a. Really? I'm from Los Angeles.
b. Really? Is she good?
c. Really? My brother's name is Jack.
d. Really? What's she like?

1. A What's your name?
    B Jack.
    A _____

2. A Where are you from?
    B San Diego.
    A _____

3. A What's your teacher like?
    B Oh, she's fun. And she plays tennis.
    A _____

4. A Who's your best friend?
    B Her name's Jill. She's a friend from high school.
    A _____

About you B Ask and answer the questions above. Give your own answers.

3 Listening and strategies Friends

A ◀)) 1.42 Listen to four people talk about people they know. Complete the chart.

	Who is it?	What's he or she like?	How old is he or she?
1. Jane	*a neighbor*	_____	_____
2. Lucas	_____	_____	_____
3. Lisa	_____	_____	_____
4. Patrick	_____	_____	_____

B ◀)) 1.42 Listen again. Choose the best way to respond to the speakers' last comments to show interest. Number the comments 1 to 4.

☐ A soccer fan? Really? Who's his favorite team?

☐ Really? So what are her songs like?

☐ Really? So is she very quiet?

☐ An art student? Really? Is he good?

About you C Pair work Write the names of three people you know on a piece of paper. Exchange lists with a partner. Ask questions about the people on your partner's list.

Chung Dae
Angela
Roberto

A **Who's Chung Dae?**
B **He's my classmate.**
A **Really? Where's he from?**

Free talk p. 130

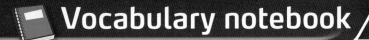

Learning tip *Making diagrams*

Make diagrams with new vocabulary. An example of a diagram is the family tree below.

In conversation

Mom or *Mother*?

▬▬▬▬▬▬	*Mom*
▬▬▬▬▬	*Mother*
▬▬▬▬	*Dad*
▬▬▬▬	*Father*
▬▬▬	*Grandma*
▬▬▬	*Grandmother*
▬	*Grandpa*
▬▬	*Grandfather*

1 Complete the family tree using the words in the box.

aunt	cousin	grandfather	mother	uncle
brother	✓father	grandmother	sister	

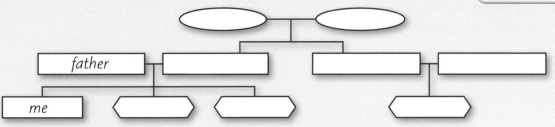

father

me

2 Now make your own family tree. Write notes about each person.

His name is Antonio.
He's forty-five.

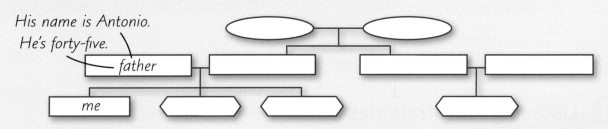

father

me

On your own

Make a photo album of your family and friends. Write sentences about them in English.

He's my grandfather.
He's very smart.

Can Do! Now I can . . .

✓ I can . . .   ? I need to review how to . . .

- ☐ talk about my favorite celebrities.
- ☐ describe people's personalities.
- ☐ ask and answer *yes-no* questions.
- ☐ talk about family members.
- ☐ say people's ages.

- ☐ ask and answer information questions.
- ☐ understand people talking about friends (ages, interests, etc.).
- ☐ show I'm interested in a conversation or surprised.

1 Can you complete this conversation?

Complete the conversation with the words in the box. Use capital letters when necessary.
Then practice with a partner.

is	
✓ are	
am	
I'm	
you're	
he's	
it's	
we're	
they're	
his	
her	
my	
your	
our	
their	
this	
these	

Angel Hi, Carla. How ___are___ you?

Carla _____ fine, thanks. Is _____ your car?

Angel No. _____ my brother's car. _____ on vacation.

Carla Cool. So where is _____ brother?

Angel He and _____ wife are in Miami, with her parents. _____ family _____ from Miami, you know.

Carla Oh, right. So are _____ children in Miami, too?

Angel No, _____ with my parents and me. _____ house is crazy. _____ all so busy with the kids.

Carla I bet _____ tired.

Angel Yeah, I really _____ . . . . Uh-oh, I'm late!

Carla OK. See you later.

Angel Wait! Where are my keys? I mean, where are _____ brother's keys?

Carla Are _____ his keys? Under the car? Here you go.

Angel Oh, thanks, Carla. You're wonderful!

2 Can you unscramble the questions?

Put the words in the correct order to make questions. Then ask and answer
the questions with a partner.

1. teacher's / last / is / our / name / What / ?
   What is our teacher's last name?

2. from / grandparents / your / Where / are / ?
   _____

3. class / hard / our / English / Is / ?
   _____

4. are / in this class / students / like / What / the / ?
   _____

5. today / not / Who's / in class / ?
   _____

6. bags / are / Where / students' / the / ?
   _____

3 How many words do you remember?

Complete the chart. Then make questions to ask and answer with a partner.

Classroom items	Locations in class	Family and other people	Words to describe people
teacher's desk	on the wall	neighbors	friendly

"Where's the teacher's desk?"   "What's on the wall?"

"What are your neighbors like?"   "Are your neighbors friendly?"

4 Do you know these expressions?

Complete the conversation with expressions from the box. Then practice with a partner.

Thank you.   Thanks anyway.   Nice to meet you.   ✓Can I borrow your pen?   Really?
That's OK.   You're welcome.   Have a good day.   How do you spell *neighbor*?   How about you?

Anna   Oh, no! Where's my pen? . . . Excuse me.
<u>Can I borrow your pen</u>   ?

Michel Sure. Here you go.

Anna   _____ .

Michel You're welcome.

Anna   Hmm . . . _____ ?

Michel *Neighbor?* I'm sorry. I don't know.

Anna   That's OK. _____ .

Michel Wait. There's a dictionary app on my tablet.

Anna   Oh, thank you!

Michel _____ .

Anna   Oh. This is a French-English dictionary.

Michel Yes. I'm from France.

Anna   France? _____ ?
Are you from Paris?

Michel Yeah, I am. _____ ?

Anna   I'm from New York. Uh-oh! My coffee!
I'm sorry.

Michel _____ .

Anna   By the way, my name is Anna.

Michel I'm Michel. _____ .

Anna   Oh, no. I'm late for work. Sorry. Bye.
_____ .

Michel Thanks. You too. . . . Uh-oh. Where's
my pen?

5 Who has the same answer?

A Complete questions 1 to 3 with *'s* or *s'* and questions 4 to 8 with question words and *be*.
Write your answers.

	Your answer	Classmates with the same answer
1. What's your best friend <u>'s</u> name?	_____	_____
2. What are your parent _____ names?	_____	_____
3. What's your mother _____ first name?	_____	_____
4. _____ your best friend? 20? 21?	_____	_____
5. _____ your best friend like?	_____	_____
6. _____ your parents now? At work?	_____	_____
7. _____ your favorite singers?	_____	_____
8. _____ your favorite TV show?	_____	_____

B **Class activity** Ask your classmates the questions. Who has the same answer?

Everyday life

☑ Can Do! In this unit, you learn how to . . .

Lesson A
- Describe a typical morning using the simple present

Lesson B
- Describe weekly routines
- Ask and answer *yes-no* questions about your week

Lesson C
- Say more than *yes* or *no* to be friendly
- Say *Well* to get more time to think

Lesson D
- Read an article about American habits
- Write about a classmate for a class website

Before you begin . . .

Match each activity with a picture. Which activities do you do every day?

☐ do homework	☐ exercise	☐ have coffee
1 work	☐ watch TV	☐ check email

What's a typical morning like in your home?

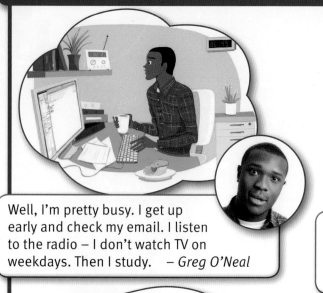

Well, I'm pretty busy. I get up early and check my email. I listen to the radio – I don't watch TV on weekdays. Then I study.   – Greg O'Neal

Noisy! I try to study, but my brother and sister make a lot of noise. They don't care. My sister watches TV, and my brother plays games on the computer.   – Jennifer Lee

It's crazy. We get up late, so I eat breakfast in the car. My husband doesn't have breakfast – he drives.   – Amanda Sanchez

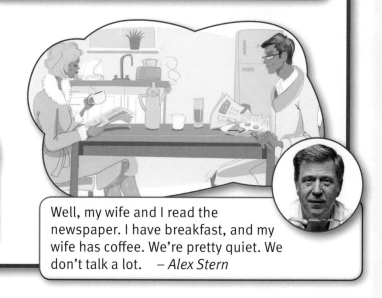

Well, my wife and I read the newspaper. I have breakfast, and my wife has coffee. We're pretty quiet. We don't talk a lot.   – Alex Stern

1 Getting started

About you **A** Look at the pictures. Check (✓) the things you do in the morning. Add your own ideas.

- ☐ get up early
- ☐ eat breakfast
- ☐ listen to the radio
- ☐ drive to work
- ☐ go on the Internet
- ☐ play games on the computer

B 🔊 1.43 Listen and read. Are you like any of these people?

Figure it out **C** What do the people above say about their mornings? Can you complete their sentences?

1. Greg   I _____ to the radio. I _____ _____ TV.

2. Alex   My wife and I _____ the newspaper. We _____ _____ a lot.

3. Jennifer   My brother and sister _____ a lot of noise. They _____ _____ .

4. Amanda   My husband _____ to work. He _____ _____ breakfast.

2 Grammar Simple present statements ◀))) 1.44

Extra practice p. 142

I **eat**	breakfast.
You **have**	coffee.
We **get up**	late.
They **read**	the paper.
He **listens**	to the radio.
She **watches**	TV.

I **don't eat**	lunch.
You **don't have**	tea.
We **don't get up**	early.
They **don't read**	books.
He **doesn't listen**	to CDs.
She **doesn't watch**	videos.

don't = do not   doesn't = does not

Verb endings: *he, she,* and *it*

get	▶	gets
watch	▶	watches
play	▶	plays
study	▶	studies
have	▶	has
do	▶	does
go	▶	goes

In conversation

Don't and *doesn't* are more common than *do not* and *does not.*

■ *does not*
■■■ *doesn't*
■ *do not*
■■■■ *don't*

A Complete the sentences. Compare answers with a partner.

1. I ___*get up*___ (get up) early every morning.
   I _*don't get up*_ (not / get up) late.

2. In my family, we _____ (have) breakfast together,
   but we _____ (not / talk) a lot.

3. My mother just _____ (have) coffee.
   She _____ (not / eat) in the morning.

4. My sister _____ (study) in the morning. She _____ (do) her homework.

5. My brother _____ (go) on the Internet. Then he _____ (watch) TV.

6. My parents _____ (not / watch) TV. They _____ (read) the newspaper.

About you B Write five sentences about your mornings. Compare with a partner.

I get up early every morning.

▶ A *I get up early every morning. How about you?*
   B *I don't get up early. I get up late.*

3 Speaking naturally -s endings of verbs

| /s/ like**s** get**s** | /z/ listen**s** stud**ies** | /ɪz/ relax**es** watch**es** |

A ◀))) 1.45 Listen and repeat the words above. Notice the verb endings.

B ◀))) 1.46 Listen to these sentences. Do the verbs end in /s/or /z/, or do they add the syllable /ɪz/? Check (✓) the correct column. Listen again and repeat.

	/s/-/z/	/ɪz/		/s/-/z/	/ɪz/
1. My mom sings in the shower.	✓		5. My brother goes on the Internet.		
2. My dad gets up early.			6. My co-worker checks his email.		
3. My mom uses an alarm clock.			7. My sister likes mornings.		
4. My friend exercises in the morning.			8. My dad relaxes on the weekends.		

About you C Pair work Talk about your family and friends and what they do in the mornings.

"My mom likes mornings. She sings in the shower."

1 Building vocabulary

A 🔊 1.47 Listen and say the expressions. Then check (✓) the things you do every week. Can you add more activities?

☐ take a class

☐ clean the house

☐ play sports

☐ go shopping

☐ do the laundry

☐ make phone calls

Word sort **B** For each day of the week, write one thing you usually do. Then tell the class.

Sunday	Monday	Tuesday	Wednesday	Thursday	Friday	Saturday
	play soccer					

"I play soccer on Mondays."

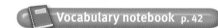
Vocabulary notebook p. 42

2 Building language

A 🔊 1.48 Listen to the questionnaire. Complete the questions and answers. Listen again and circle the answers that are true for you.

What's your weekly routine?

1. Do you take a class in the evening?   Yes, I do.   No, I don't.
2. Do you and your family eat together on Sundays?   Yes, we do.   No, we don't.
3. Do your friends call you in the evening?   Yes, they do.   No, they don't.
4. Does your best friend meet you after class?   Yes, he / she does.   No, he / she doesn't.

Figure it out

5. _____ you and your friends _____ sports?   Yes, _____ .   No, _____ .
6. _____ you _____ shopping on Saturdays?   Yes, _____ .   No, _____ .
7. _____ your best friend _____ shopping with you? Yes, _____ .   No, _____ .

About you **B** **Pair work** Ask and answer the questions above. Can you give more information?

A *Do you take a class in the evening?*

B *Yes, I do. I go to an English class.*

3 Grammar *Yes-no* questions and short answers 🔊 1.49

Extra practice p. 142

Do you **go** to a class in the evening?   Yes, I **do**.   No, I **don't**.
Do you and your friends **play** sports after class? Yes, we **do**.   No, we **don't**.
Do your friends **make** phone calls at night?   Yes, they **do**. No, they **don't**.
Does your mother **work** on the weekends?   Yes, she **does**. No, she **doesn't**.

Time expressions

on Monday(s)
on (the) weekend(s)
in the morning(s)
in the afternoon(s)
in the evening(s)
at night
before breakfast
after class
every day

✖ Common errors

In short answers, do not use a verb after *don't* or *doesn't*.

Do you have a computer?
*No, I **don't**.*
(NOT ~~No, I don't have.~~)

A Complete the questions. Compare with a partner.

1. ___Do___ you __make__ phone calls late at night?
2. _____ your friends _____ on the Internet in class?
3. _____ your mother _____ her email every day?
4. _____ your parents _____ the laundry on weekends?
5. _____ your father _____ the news online every day?
6. _____ you and your friends _____ online games together?
7. _____ your best friend _____ classes in the evenings?
8. _____ you _____ shopping after class?
9. _____ your family _____ breakfast together in the morning?
10. _____ you _____ your room every day?

About you **B Pair work** Ask and answer the questions. How many of your answers are the same?

A *Do you make phone calls late at night?*
B *No, I don't. I go to bed early every night.*

4 Class survey Who has a busy week?

A Write questions to ask your classmates. Compare with a partner.

Find someone who . . .	Ask . . .	Name
1. exercises before breakfast.	*Do you exercise before breakfast?*	_____
2. cleans the house every day.	_____	_____
3. studies English late at night.	_____	_____
4. gets up early on Sundays.	_____	_____
5. plays on a sports team.	_____	_____
6. works on the weekends.	_____	_____
7. goes to bed early every night.	_____	_____
8. eats a snack after class.	_____	_____

About you **B Class activity** Find classmates who do the things in the chart above. Write their names in the chart.

A *Do you exercise before breakfast?*
B *Yes, I do. I go to the gym before breakfast.*

C Pair work Tell your partner something interesting about a classmate.

"Yoshiko goes to the gym before breakfast."

1 Conversation strategy Saying more than *yes* or *no*

A Look at the photo. What do you think Celia and Andy are talking about?

B 🔊 1.50 Listen. What do you find out about Celia? How about Andy?

Celia	Hi. I see you here all the time. Do you work out every day?
Andy	Well, I come here before class.
Celia	Oh, are you a student?
Andy	Yeah. Well, I'm a part-time law student. And I work at a TV station, too.
Celia	A TV station? Really?
Andy	Yeah. I'm an intern. So, do you come here every day?
Celia	Uh-huh. I run here from home every morning.
Andy	Oh, so do you live around here?
Celia	No. I live about 10 miles away.
Andy	So you run 10 miles a day? Wow!

C Notice how Andy and Celia answer questions. They say more than *yes* or *no*. They want to be friendly. Find examples in the conversation.

"Oh, so do you live around here?"
"No. I live about 10 miles away."

D Find two good answers for each question below. Write the letters *a* to *h*. Compare with a partner.

1. Do you live around here?   _c_ ___
2. Do you have a job?   ___ ___
3. Are you from here originally?   ___ ___
4. Do you have brothers and sisters? ___ ___

a. Well, I work at a store on the weekends.
b. No, I'm from Chicago originally.
c. Well, I live about two miles away.
d. No, I'm an only child.
e. No, I don't. I live in Oaktown.
f. Yeah. I have a part-time job at a restaurant.
g. Yes, I am. But my parents are from Turkey.
h. Yes, I have a sister.

About you **E Pair work** Ask and answer the questions above with a partner. Give your own answers, and say more than *yes* or *no*.

A *Do you live around here?*
B *No, I don't. I live about seven miles away.*

2 Strategy plus *Well, . . .*

Start your answer with *Well* if you need time to think, or if your answer is not a simple *yes* or *no*.

Do you work out every day?

Well, I come here before class.

A 🔊 **1.51 Match the questions with the responses. Then listen and check your answers. Practice with a partner.**

In conversation

Well is one of the top 50 words.

1. Are you from a big family? __e__
2. Do you work out a lot? _____
3. Do you like sports? _____
4. Do you study every day? _____
5. Who's your favorite actor? _____

a. Well, I don't play sports, but I watch soccer on TV.
b. Well, not every day. I go to the gym two days a week.
c. Well, I like a lot of actors. I don't have a favorite actor.
d. Well, not every day. I don't study on the weekends.
e. Well, I have two brothers and a sister.

About you **B Pair work Ask and answer the questions above. Give your own answers.**

3 Listening and strategies Casual conversations

A 🔊 **1.52 Can you guess the missing words in these conversations? Listen and write what the people say. Then practice.**

1. A Do you text your _____ ?
   B No, not really. Well, on my way home _____ . I text and say "I'm on my way."

2. A Do you watch a lot of sports on TV?
   B Well, I only watch _____ . You know, _____ .

3. A Do you read the news _____ ?
   B Yeah. Well, _____ . I make _____ and check the headlines.

4. A Do you _____ on the Internet?
   B Yes. Well, I play chess with my friend _____ .

5. A Do you listen to the radio?
   B Well, I listen to the same show _____ . But that's all.

About you **B Pair work Take turns asking the questions above. Give your own answers.**

  A *Do you text your parents?*
  B *No, not really. Well, on my way home at night. I text and say "I'm on my way."*

1 Reading

About you **A** How much time do you spend on these activities every day? Tell the class.

- at work or school
- on the bus or train or in the car
- on the Internet
- on the phone

"I spend about an hour a day on the phone."

B Read the article and take the quiz. Then compare with a partner. Are you like average Americans?

> **Reading tip**
>
> Before you read an article, "skim" it (look at it quickly). This gives you an idea of the topics it covers.

`http://www.surveysyoulike...` [+]   Q   [−][□][X]

Are you like an average American?

Do you work eight hours a day? Then you're similar to the typical American. In fact, the average American with a full-time job works just over eight hours a day. How much time do you spend on the Internet? The average American spends just under two and a half hours a day online.

So do you live your life like the average American? Find out with our quiz.

Quiz	Average American	You	
1. Do you get up at 6:30 a.m. on weekdays?	Yes	Yes ○	No ○
2. Do you sing in the shower?	No	Yes ○	No ○
3. Do you have cereal with milk for breakfast?	Yes	Yes ○	No ○
4. Do you have a pet?	No	Yes ○	No ○
5. Do you use public transportation every day?	No	Yes ○	No ○
6. Do you watch television about three hours a day?	Yes	Yes ○	No ○
7. Do you exercise every day?	No	Yes ○	No ○
8. Do you eat at a restaurant three times a week?	Yes	Yes ○	No ○

So are you like the average American? If you're not, that's OK – it's fun to compare your life with the lives of people in another country. If you are, that's OK too, because the average American is happy!

C Read the article again. What does it say about these things? Check (✓) *True* (T) or *False* (F).

The average American . . .	T	F
1. works under 10 hours a day.	✓	☐
2. spends three and a half hours on the Internet every day.	☐	☐
3. gets up at 8:00 a.m. on weekdays.	☐	☐
4. eats cereal in the morning.	☐	☐
5. eats at a restaurant about four times a week.	☐	☐
6. uses public transportation every day.	☐	☐

))) **Sounds right** p. 137

2 Listening Teen habits

A ◀)) 1.53 Read about the habits of an average teenager in the United States. Then listen to an interview with teenager Tyler Johnson. Complete the sentences about Tyler.

An average teenager . . .	Tyler Johnson . . .
• sends or receives over 200 text messages a day.	1. sends _____ text messages a day.
• listens to music for 2 hours every day.	2. listens to music for _____ hours every day.
• spends over 4 hours a day on the Internet.	3. spends _____ hours a day on the Internet.
• watches TV about 20 hours a week.	4. watches TV about _____ hours a week.

About you **B** ◀)) 1.54 Listen to some of Tyler's statements again. Are you like Tyler, or are you different? Check the correct box. Compare with a partner.

	1	2	3	4
I'm just like Tyler.	☐	☐	☐	☐
I'm different from Tyler.	☐	☐	☐	☐

3 Writing and speaking A typical week

A Complete the sentences. Then tell a partner about your typical week. Take notes on your partner's typical week.

A typical week for me	A typical week for my partner
I take classes _____ hours a week.	_____
I work / study _____ hours a week.	_____
I spend _____ hours a week on the Internet.	_____
I watch TV _____ hours a week.	_____
I spend _____ hours a week with my friends.	_____

B Read about a student on a class website. Circle the capital letters. Find a rule for each circled letter in the Help note.

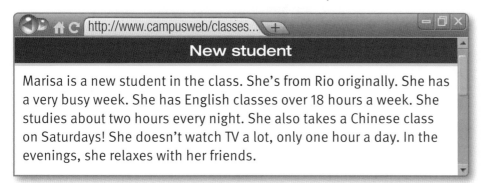

Marisa is a new student in the class. She's from Rio originally. She has a very busy week. She has English classes over 18 hours a week. She studies about two hours every night. She also takes a Chinese class on Saturdays! She doesn't watch TV a lot, only one hour a day. In the evenings, she relaxes with her friends.

Help note

Capitals and periods
Use CAPITAL letters for
  • new sentences.
  • people's names.
  • names of places.
  • names of languages.
  • days of the week.
Use a period (.) at the end of your sentences.

C Write a profile about your partner. Use your notes from above to help you.

D Pair work Read your partner's profile. Ask three questions for more information.   Free talk p. 130

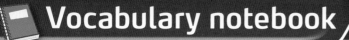

Vocabulary notebook / Verbs, verbs, verbs

Learning tip *Drawing pictures*

Draw and label simple pictures in your notebook. The pictures below show different verbs.

1 Label the pictures. Use a verb to describe each activity.

| *read the newspaper* | | | |

2 Draw and label your own pictures of activities.

| | | | |

3 Complete the chart with your everyday activities.

Write two things you do . . .		
every day	*I read the newspaper.*	
in the afternoon		
on Sundays		
after breakfast		
before bed		

 On your own

Write labels for the things you do every day. Put your labels around the house.

Can Do! Now I can . . .

| ✓ I can . . . | ? I need to review how to . . . |

- [ ] describe a typical morning.
- [ ] ask questions about weekly routines.
- [ ] answer questions with more than *yes* or *no* to be friendly.
- [ ] say *Well* to get time to think and to answer questions.

- [ ] understand conversations about routines.
- [ ] understand an interview about habits.
- [ ] read an article about the average American.
- [ ] write about a classmate for a class website.

Free time

5

☑ **Can Do!** In this unit, you learn how to . . .

Lesson A
- Talk about your free time
- Ask simple present information questions

Lesson B
- Say how often you do things
- Talk about TV shows you like

Lesson C
- Ask questions in two ways to be clear or not too direct
- Say *I mean* to say more or repeat ideas

Lesson D
- Read an article on technology addicts
- Email a friend for advice using *and* and *but*

1. go to the movies

2. eat out

3. go to a club

4. go on the Internet

Before you begin . . .
- Do you do these things every day?
- . . . every week?
- . . . once a month?

43

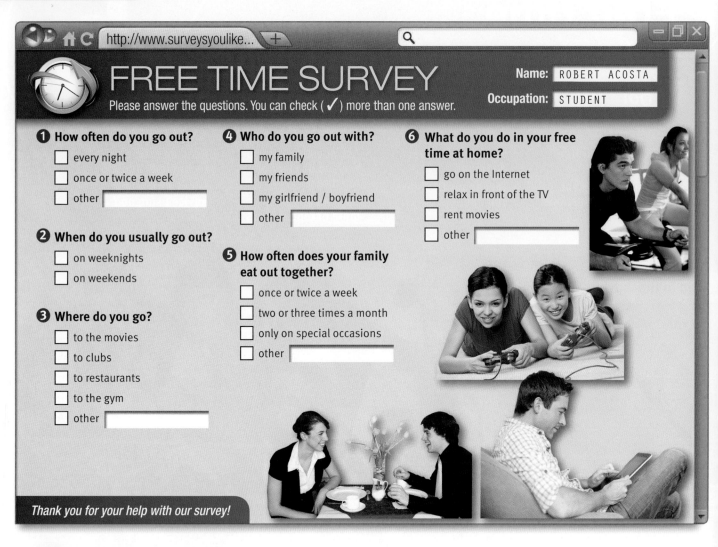

http://www.surveysyoulike...

FREE TIME SURVEY

Name: ROBERT ACOSTA
Occupation: STUDENT

Please answer the questions. You can check (✓) more than one answer.

❶ How often do you go out?
- [ ] every night
- [ ] once or twice a week
- [ ] other

❷ When do you usually go out?
- [ ] on weeknights
- [ ] on weekends

❸ Where do you go?
- [ ] to the movies
- [ ] to clubs
- [ ] to restaurants
- [ ] to the gym
- [ ] other

❹ Who do you go out with?
- [ ] my family
- [ ] my friends
- [ ] my girlfriend / boyfriend
- [ ] other

❺ How often does your family eat out together?
- [ ] once or twice a week
- [ ] two or three times a month
- [ ] only on special occasions
- [ ] other

❻ What do you do in your free time at home?
- [ ] go on the Internet
- [ ] relax in front of the TV
- [ ] rent movies
- [ ] other

Thank you for your help with our survey!

1 Getting started

A What activities do you do in your free time? Tell the class.

"I play soccer."   *"I go to the gym."*

B 🔊 **2.01** Listen and read as Robert completes the survey with his friend Rebecca. Check (✓) his answers.

C Put the words in the correct order to make questions. Use the survey to help you. Then practice with a partner.

1. A you / do / When / go out / ?
   B I go out on weekends.

2. A Who / you / do / go out with / ?
   B I go out with my friends.

3. A What / in your free time / do / you / do / ?
   B I go on the Internet.

4. A your family / eat out together / How often / does / ?
   B Twice a month.

About you **D** **Pair work** Ask and answer the questions in the survey. Complete the survey for your partner.

44

2 Grammar Simple present information questions ◀)) 2.02

Extra practice p. 143

What	do	you	**do** in your free time?	Meet my friends.
Who	do	you	**go out** with?	A friend.
When	does	she	**go out**?	On the weekends.
How often	does	he	**eat out**?	Twice a month.
Where	do	they	**go** on Saturday nights?	To the movies.

How often?

every day
on Friday nights
once a week
three times a week
twice a month

A Write information questions to complete the conversations.
Then practice with a partner.

1. A I eat out once a week.
   B Really? *Where do you go* ?
   A I go to a restaurant near my house.

2. A I go to the movies on Friday nights.
   B Yeah? _____ ?
   A I go with some friends from work.

3. A My best friend texts me a lot.
   B _____ ?
   A He texts me about 20 times a day!

4. A My friend goes to the gym every day.
   B Really? _____ ?
   A She goes in the morning before work.

5. A My parents go out about once a month.
   B So _____ ?
   A Well, they go to a club or they eat out.

6. A I have a lot of free time before class.
   B Really? _____ ?
   A Oh, I go to a café and read.

7. A My sister plays sports twice a week.
   B Really? _____ ?
   A Soccer and tennis.

8. A I go out on Thursday nights.
   B _____ ?
   A My sister. We go to our favorite café.

About you **B** **Pair work** Change the underlined words in the conversations above
to your own information. Then take turns starting conversations.

A *I go to a club once a week.*
B *Really? Who do you go with?*

X Common errors

Don't forget to add *do* or *does*
before the subject.
*Where **does** she go?*
(NOT ~~Where she goes?~~)

3 Speaking naturally Do you . . . ?

Do you go out a lot?   Where **do you** go?   What **do you** do?

A ◀)) 2.03 Listen and repeat the questions above. Notice the pronunciation of *do you*.

B ◀)) 2.04 Listen and complete the conversations. Then practice with a partner.

1. A *Do you relax* in your free time?
   B Well, yes, on the weekends.
   A _____ ?
   B I sleep late, read, watch TV . . .

2. A _____ movies?
   B Yes, I do. I like movies a lot.
   A _____ ?
   B Two or three times a month.

About you **C** **Pair work** Make a survey about weekends. Write five information questions.
Then ask a partner your questions.

1 Building language

A 🔊 **2.05 Listen. When does Mandy watch TV?**
Practice the conversation.

Eric   This soup is delicious. What's in it? . . . Mandy? Mandy!
Mandy   I'm sorry, what?
Eric   You know, sometimes I think you watch too much TV.
Mandy   Oh, I hardly ever watch TV.
Eric   Are you serious?
Mandy   Well, sometimes I watch the morning shows. And I usually watch the late movie.
Eric   And you always have dinner in front of the TV! I mean, you never talk to me.
Mandy   Yes, I do! I talk to you during the commercials.

Figure it out B Complete the sentences. Find the words in the conversation.

1. Mandy   I _____ watch TV. Well, _____ I watch the morning shows.
2. Mandy   I _____ watch the late movie.
3. Eric   You _____ have dinner in front of the TV. You _____ talk to me.

2 Grammar Frequency adverbs 🔊 2.06

Extra practice p. 143

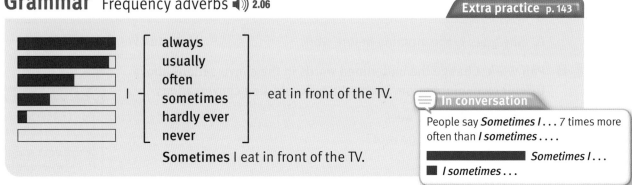

always
usually
often
I   sometimes   eat in front of the TV.
hardly ever
never

Sometimes I eat in front of the TV.

In conversation

People say **Sometimes I** . . . 7 times more often than **I sometimes** . . . .

▬▬▬▬▬▬▬▬▬ **Sometimes I** . . .
▪ **I sometimes** . . .

About you Add frequency adverbs to make true sentences. Then compare with a partner.

1. I do my homework in front of the TV.   *I never do my homework in front of the TV.*
2. I watch TV in the morning.
3. My family has dinner in front of the TV.
4. My best friend watches sports on TV.
5. My family watches movies on Friday nights.
6. I watch the news in the evening.
7. My friends and I watch TV shows in English.
8. I watch commercials on TV.

A *I never do my homework in front of the TV.*

B *Really? Sometimes I do homework in front of the TV, but not every day.*

> ✗ **Common errors**
>
> Don't put **always**, **hardly ever**, or **never** before the subject.
>
> I **always** watch the news.
> (NOT ~~Always I~~ watch the news.)

3 Building vocabulary

A 🔊 2.07 Listen. What kinds of TV shows do you hear? Number the shows 1 to 8.

☐ cartoon

☐ soap opera

☐ talk show

☐ game show

☐ documentary

☐ reality show

☐ sitcom

☐ the news

Word sort **B** What kinds of shows do you like and dislike? Complete the chart. Add other kinds of shows.

Likes	Dislikes
I love _reality shows_ .	I hate _____ .
I really like _____ .	I can't stand _____ .
I like _____ .	I don't like _____ .

About you **C** **Pair work** What kinds of TV shows does your partner like? Ask about each type of show above.

A *Do you like reality shows?*

B *Yes, I do. I often watch reality shows. My favorite is . . .*

> **i Note**
> When you talk about your general likes and dislikes, use a plural noun.
> *I like cartoons and sitcoms.*

Vocabulary notebook p. 52

4 Talk about it How much TV do you watch?

A **Pair work** Discuss the questions. How are you and your partner the same? How are you different? Take notes on your partner's answers.

▶ How many hours of TV do you watch a week?
▶ How often do you watch TV in bed?
▶ Do you ever fall asleep in front of the TV?
▶ How often do you watch TV on your computer?
▶ Do you watch TV on your phone or tablet?
▶ Do you think you watch too much TV?

B **Pair work** Find a new partner. Ask and answer questions about each other's first partner.

A *How often does Juan watch TV?*

B *He watches TV all the time! He watches the news in the morning and . . .*

1 Conversation strategy Asking questions in two ways

A What do people often do after class? Think of six things and make a list.

B 🔊 2.08 Listen. What does Gabby do after class?

Stan So what do you do after class? Do you go straight home?

Gabby Well, usually. Sometimes I meet a friend for dinner.

Stan Oh, where do you go? I mean, do you go somewhere nice?

Gabby Do you know Fabio's? It's OK. I mean, the food's good, and it's cheap, but the service is terrible. Do you know it?

Stan Well, actually, I work there. I'm a server.

C Notice how Stan asks questions in two ways. His questions are clear and not too direct. Find examples in the conversation.

> *"So what do you do after class? Do you go straight home?"*

D 🔊 2.09 Match the first question to a good second question. Listen and check. Then practice.

1. What do you do for lunch? __f__
2. Where do you go after class? _____
3. How often do you go shopping? _____
4. Do you go to the gym in the mornings? _____
5. Who do you hang out with from class? _____
6. How do you usually get home after class? _____
7. What's your favorite restaurant? _____
8. Do you ever feel tired after class? _____

a. Do you take the subway or the bus?
b. I mean, do you have friends in your class?
c. I mean, do you need coffee?
d. Do you have a job in the evening?
e. I mean, do you exercise before class?
f. Do you take a short break?
g. I mean, do you go every weekend?
h. I mean, do you have a favorite?

About you **E** **Pair work** Ask and answer the pairs of questions. Give your own answers.

A What do you do for lunch? Do you take a short break?

B Well, I usually go for a walk in the park and eat a sandwich.

48

2 Strategy plus *I mean*

You can use *I mean* to repeat your ideas or to say more about something.

In conversation

I mean is one of the top 15 expressions.

Where do you go? I mean, do you go somewhere nice?

Do you know Fabio's? It's OK. I mean, the food's good, . . .

A 🔊 2.10 **Complete the conversations with sentences from the box. Write *a* to *f*. Then listen and check.**

a. I mean, we have dinner and watch a movie.
b. I mean, I often go to bed early during the week.
c. I mean, they're not cheap, but they're good.
d. I mean, I have two part-time jobs.
e. I mean, are they good?
f. I mean, do you have any free time?

1. A Do you ever go out on weeknights?
    B Well, not very often. _____

2. A How do you like the restaurants around here? _____
    B They're OK. _____

3. A Do you have time to relax on the weekends?
    B Yeah. I spend time with my family. _____

4. A What do you do in your free time? _____
    B Well, I don't have a lot. _____

About you **B** **Pair work** Practice the conversations above. Then practice again giving your own answers. Use *I mean*.

A Do you ever go out on the weeknights?
B Well, sometimes. I mean, I sometimes meet a friend after class.

3 Listening and strategies What's the question?

A 🔊 2.11 **Listen to the things five people say. What questions are the people answering? Number the questions 1 to 5.**

☐ So what do you usually do in the evenings? I mean, do you spend time with your family?
☐ Where do you go on Friday nights? I mean, do you usually go to a club?
☐ Do you know your neighbors? I mean, are they nice?
☐ Who's your best friend? I mean, who do you usually hang out with?
☐ So when do you usually have free time? I mean, do you have time during the week?

About you **B** **Pair work** Ask and answer the questions above. Give your own answers.

About you **C** **Pair work** Find a new partner. Think of a different second question for each question above. Then ask and answer the questions.

"So what do you usually do in the evenings? I mean, do you watch TV?"

Free talk p. 131

Lesson D / Technology addicts

1 Reading

A Read the statements about technology. Do you agree? Tell the class.

1. Technology is great. It helps you keep in touch with people.
2. Technology is good, but people spend too much time on their computers and cell phones.

B Read the article. What do technology addicts do? Find six things.

📖 **Reading tip**

Before you read an article, read the title. Ask yourself questions.
For example:
What is a technology diet? Do I need it?

http://www.technologytopics...

Do You Need A Technology Diet?

Technology is great. We text and email friends all day long, and we're always in touch with the office. Some experts say that a lot of people are now "technology addicts" – they spend too much time on computers and phones. So how do you know if you have a problem? Answer these questions. If you answer yes to all of them, maybe you're a technology addict.

▶ What's the first thing you do in the morning? Do you check your email and text messages?

▶ Do you ever go out with one friend and then spend time talking to a different friend on your cell phone?

▶ Do you spend a lot of time on your social network and hardly ever see your friends?

▶ Do you answer calls or texts in a movie theater?

▶ How much time do you spend online every day? Is it more than six hours?

Technology *is* very useful, but if you spend all your time on your computer and your cell phone, that's not good for you or for your family or friends! Maybe you need to go on a "technology diet." What does that mean? Well, enjoy breakfast with your family. Use your social networking site, but meet your friends, too, and do something fun together. Talk to the friend you are with now. So give it a try. Turn off your phone . . . just for a minute. Like, right now?

C According to the article, what is good advice for a technology addict? What is bad advice? Check (✓) the boxes.

	Good advice	Bad advice
1. Send a lot of text messages when you're at the movies.	☐	☐
2. Meet face-to-face with family and friends.	☐	☐
3. Turn off your cell phone sometimes.	☐	☐
4. Check your email right after you get up in the morning.	☐	☐
5. Spend more time with friends and less time on social networks.	☐	☐
6. Eat meals with your family and talk.	☐	☐

2 Listening and speaking Using phones

A What do people use their phones for? How many different ideas can you think of? Tell the class.

"They go on the Internet."   *"They send text messages."*

B ◀ﺒ 2.12 Listen. How do Megan and Ryan use their phones? Check (✓) the boxes.

Megan
- ☐ She checks her email.
- ☐ She pays bills.
- ☐ She goes on her social networking site.
- ☐ She listens to music.

Ryan
- ☐ He plays games.
- ☐ He texts people.
- ☐ He calls his girlfriend.
- ☐ He takes photos.

About you **C** **Pair work** Discuss the questions. Do you and your partner use phones for the same things?

- What kind of phone do you have?
- What do you use your phone for?
- Do you send a lot of text messages?
- Who do you usually text?
- Who do you usually call?
- Do you use your phone everywhere?
- Where *don't* you use your phone?

(((·**Sounds right** p. 137

3 Writing Technology and you

A How do you use your computer or phone? Make a list of the different ways.

My computer   I check my social network five or six times a day. I don't send a lot of emails.

B Read the email and the Help note. Underline the words *and* and *but*.

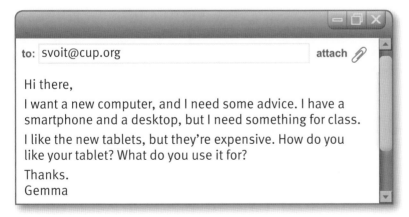

to: svoit@cup.org   attach

Hi there,
I want a new computer, and I need some advice. I have a smartphone and a desktop, but I need something for class.
I like the new tablets, but they're expensive. How do you like your tablet? What do you use it for?
Thanks.
Gemma

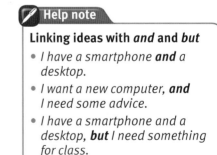

Help note

Linking ideas with *and* and *but*
- *I have a smartphone **and** a desktop.*
- *I want a new computer, **and** I need some advice.*
- *I have a smartphone and a desktop, **but** I need something for class.*

C Write a reply to the email above. Use *and* and *but* to link your ideas. Then read your classmates' replies. Do they give the same advice as you?

About you **D** **Pair work** Take the quiz in the article with a partner. Ask and answer the questions. Does your partner need a technology diet? Do you?

Learning tip *Verbs + . . .*

Write down verbs and the words you can use *after* them.

	play music
	sports
	soccer

1 Which words and expressions in the box go with the verbs below? Complete the chart.

a class	dinner	lessons	✓music	snacks	the laundry
breakfast	homework	lunch	on a team	soccer	video games

play	*music*	eat		take		do	

2 Now think of words and expressions that go with these verbs.

go	*to a class*	watch	*documentaries*	read	
	out				

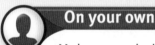
On your own

Make a vocabulary "flip pad."
On each page, write a verb with
words you can use after it. Look
through it when you have time.

stand in line

Can Do! Now I can . . .

✓ I can . . .   ? I need to review how to . . .

- ☐ ask and answer questions about my free time.
- ☐ say how often I do things.
- ☐ talk about the TV shows I like and don't like.
- ☐ ask a question in two ways to be clear or not too direct.

- ☐ use *I mean* to say more or repeat ideas.
- ☐ understand the main topics in everyday conversations.
- ☐ understand a conversation about cell phones.
- ☐ read an article about technology addicts.
- ☐ write an email to a friend to ask for advice.

Neighborhoods

✓ Can Do! **In this unit, you learn how to . . .**

Lesson A
- Say what's in a neighborhood with *There's / There are*
- Describe places

Lesson B
- Tell the time and ask questions with *What time . . . ?*
- Make suggestions with *Let's*

Lesson C
- Say *Me too* or *Me neither* to show things in common
- Say *Right* or *I know* to agree

Lesson D
- Read a guide to New York City
- Write a city guide using prepositions

2. a stadium

1. a mall

4. a museum

PEROT MUSEUM OF NATURE AND SCIENCE

3. a park

Before you begin . . .

- What do people do at these places?
- Do you have places like these in your city?
- How often do you go to them?

How do you like your neighborhood?

People talk about the popular neighborhood called Parkview.

HOME   LATEST POST   TOP POSTS

Amy Johnson, 32, medical researcher

Well, Parkview is convenient. There's a big supermarket and some nice stores, but there's no mall. We need a mall!

Paul Johnson, 33, stockbroker

Um, it's nice. There are two nice outdoor cafés and a couple of movie theaters. There's a new swimming pool in the park – we have a beautiful little park. Yeah, it's good.

Stacy King, 19, college student

Parkview is boring! There's no place to go. I mean, there's no mall, no fast-food places – just a lot of expensive restaurants. Oh, and a small park.

1 Getting started

A Look at the map of Parkview. Check (✓) the places you see. What other places do you see?

☐ an apartment building   ☐ a supermarket   ☐ a mall   ☐ a movie theater
☐ an outdoor café   ☐ a fast-food place   ☐ a swimming pool   ☐ a post office

B 2.13 Listen and read. Who likes Parkview? Why?

Figure it out **C** Circle the correct words to complete the sentences. Use the posts above to help you.

1. **There's / There are** a big supermarket.
2. **There's / There are** two nice outdoor cafés.
3. There's **no / some** mall.
4. Parkview has a lot of expensive **restaurant / restaurants**.
5. It has a couple of movie **theaters / theater**.

2 Grammar *There's* and *There are*; quantifiers ◀)) 2.14

Extra practice p. 144

Singular	There's	**a** park in my neighborhood.
	There's	**an** outdoor café.
	There's	**no** mall.
Plural	There are	**a lot of** restaurant**s**.
	There are	**some** outdoor café**s**.
	There are	**a couple of** movie theater**s**.
	There are	**no** club**s**.

There's = There is

Adjectives before nouns
There's a **small** park.
There's a **beautiful** pool.
There's a **new** restaurant.
There are some **expensive** stores.

In conversation

People often say *There's* before plural nouns, but it is not correct to write this.

A What else can you say about Parkview? Look at the map on page 54 and match the two parts of the sentences. Compare with a partner.

1. There's a __d__
2. There's no _____
3. There are no _____
4. There are a couple of _____
5. There are a lot of _____

a. expensive restaurants.
b. big apartment buildings.
c. stadium.
d. small gym.
e. clubs.

About you **B** Add adjectives to these sentences. Change *a* or *an* if necessary. Then make the sentences true for your neighborhood. Compare ideas with a partner.

       good
1. There are no͜ movie theaters around here. (good)
2. There are a lot of fast-food places. (cheap)
3. There are a couple of clubs. (fun)

4. There's a museum. (interesting)
5. There's no subway station. (convenient)
6. There's an outdoor café. (nice)

"There's a big movie theater in my neighborhood."

✗ Common errors

Don't add *"s"* to adjectives.

There are some nice cafés.
(NOT ~~nices~~ cafés)

3 Speaking naturally Word stress

●•
movie

●••
stadium

•●•
apartment

A ◀)) 2.15 Listen and repeat the words above. Notice the word stress.

B ◀)) 2.16 Listen and repeat these words. Then write the words in the correct column.

✓movie	beautiful
✓stadium	convenient
✓apartment	building
museum	noisy
expensive	theater
neighborhood	boring

1. ●•	2. ●••	3. •●•
movie	_stadium_	_apartment_
_____	_____	_____
_____	_____	_____
_____	_____	_____

About you **C** Pair work Use the words above to describe a perfect neighborhood. What's there? What's not there? Make a list of five places in your perfect neighborhood. Then tell the class.

"Well, there are a lot of great cafés in our perfect neighborhood."

1 Building vocabulary

A 🔊 2.17 Listen and say the times. What time is it now?

It's eleven (**o'clock**).

It's two-oh-five.
It's five **after** two.

It's four-fifteen.
It's **a quarter after** four.

It's ten-thirty.

It's six-forty-five.
It's **a quarter to** seven.

It's eight-fifty.
It's ten **to** nine.

It's twelve **a.m.**
It's **midnight**.

It's twelve **p.m.**
It's **noon**.

B Pair work Take turns asking and telling the time.

1.
2.
3.
4.
5.
6.
7.
8.

A What time is it?
B It's five-fifteen. **OR** *It's a quarter after five.*

> **ℹ Note**
> a.m. = **before** 12 noon
> p.m. = **after** 12 noon

> 💬 **In conversation**
> People say (hour)-*fifteen* more than *a quarter after* (hour).
>
> ■■■■■■ two-fifteen
> ■ a quarter after two

📓 **Vocabulary notebook** p. 62

2 Listening What's on this weekend?

🔊 2.18 How often do you go to events like these? Tell the class. Then listen to the radio show and complete the chart.

Event	Where is it?	What time does it start?
1. concert		
2. soccer match		
3. art exhibit		
4. play		

3 Building language

A 🔊 **2.19** Listen. What time is the concert? Practice the conversation.

Kyle Hey Erin, there's a free concert at the park tonight.

Erin Really? That sounds like fun. What time does it start?

Kyle It starts at 7:30.

Erin Well, let's go. What time is it now?

Kyle Um, it's 5:30. What time do you finish?

Erin About 6:00. So, let's meet there about 7:00.

Kyle Well, they don't usually have a lot of seats, so . . .

Erin Oh, well, in that case, let's get there early – say, around 6:45?

Figure it out **B** Can you complete the conversations? Use the conversation above to help you. Then practice with a partner.

1. A _____ the concert start?

   B It starts _____ 7:00.

2. A Let's _____ to a movie tonight.

   B OK. _____ meet at the theater at 6:30.

4 Grammar Questions with *What time*; suggestions with *Let's* 🔊 2.20   **Extra practice** p. 144

What time is it?	It's **6:30**.	**Suggestions**
What time does the concert start?	It starts **at** nine o'clock.	**Let's go** to the concert.
What time do supermarkets close?	**(At) about** 10:00 p.m.	**Let's meet** at 6:45.
What time do you go out at night?	Usually **around** 8:00 or 8:30.	**Let's get** there early.

In conversation

You can ask people you don't know
Excuse me, do you have the time?

A Complete the questions using *What time* and *do* or *does*. Complete the suggestions with *Let's*.

1. A Hey, there's a jazz concert on Saturday.

   B Really? *What time does* it start?

   A It starts at 8:00 p.m.

2. A _____ have dinner after the concert.

   B OK. But _____ restaurants close around here?

   A Oh, around midnight.

3. A _____ go to the pool tomorrow.

   B Great! _____ it open?

   A I think it opens early, like around 7:00 a.m.

4. A _____ meet for breakfast on Saturday.

   B OK. _____ you get up on weekends?

   A Oh, I usually get up at about 8:00.

B **Pair work** Practice the conversations. Practice again changing the times.

About you **C** **Pair work** Talk about three events this week. Make plans to go to an event together. Use the conversations above to help you.

   A *Let's go to the soccer game at the stadium tomorrow night.*

   B *OK. What time does it start?*

57

1 Conversation strategy *Me too* and *Me neither*

A Look at the photo. Can you guess the topic of Omar and Carly's conversation?

B 🔊 2.21 Listen. What's the café like?

Omar	What time is it?
Carly	11:30. Are you hungry? I'm starving.
Omar	Me too. I don't usually have breakfast in the mornings.
Carly	No, me neither. Do you know any good places to eat around here?
Omar	Well, there's a new café over there. It looks kind of nice.
Carly	Right. But I bet it's expensive. Let's try somewhere else.
Omar	I know. But don't worry – it's on me today.
Carly	Oh. Well, in that case, let's go there!

C **Notice** how Omar and Carly say *Me too* and *Me neither* to show they have something in common. Find the examples in the conversation.

"I'm starving."

"Me too."

D Write *me too* or *me neither* to complete the conversations. Then practice with a partner.

1. A I'm really hungry.
    B Yeah, *me too*   .

2. A I don't have a lot of money with me.
    B _____ .

3. A I never go to expensive restaurants.
    B No, _____ .

4. A Sometimes I eat at fast-food places.
    B Yeah, _____ .

5. A I don't often have lunch at home.
    B _____ .

6. A I really like outdoor cafés.
    B Oh, _____ .

About you **E** **Pair work** Make the sentences above true for you. Then take turns saying your sentences and responding.

A *I'm not very hungry right now.*
B *Me neither.* **OR** *Really? I'm starving.*

2 Strategy plus *Right* and *I know*

Say *Right* and *I know* to show
you agree with someone or
that you are listening.

In conversation

Right is one of the top 50 words,
and *know* is one of the top 20.

Well, there's a new
café over there. It
looks kind of nice.

I know.

Right. But I bet it's expensive.

About you Complete the sentences about the neighborhood you are in right now. Circle the words
or add your own ideas. Then take turns saying your sentences and responding.

1. This is ~~an exciting~~ / ~~a boring~~ / *an interesting* neighborhood.
2. There are a lot of **interesting buildings** / **museums** / _____ around here.
3. There's no **mall** / **subway** / _____ .
4. The neighborhood needs a nice **outdoor café** / **swimming pool** / _____ .
5. I don't like the **clubs** / **movie theaters** / _____ here.
6. There are some very **cheap** / **expensive** / _____ stores.

A This is an interesting neighborhood.

B Right. There are some nice cafés around here. OR Really? I don't think it's very interesting.

3 Listening and strategies Let's go there!

((· Sounds right p. 137

A ((») 2.22 Listen. Where do the people decide to go? Circle *a* or *b*.

1. Jason and Sophia choose a place   a. to shop.   b. to eat.
2. Tyler and Jen choose a place   a. to have fun.   b. to study.
3. Michael and Anna choose a place   a. to exercise.   b. to eat.

About you **B ((») 2.23** Listen to three statements from the conversations. Are you the same or different?
Check (✓) the column you agree with. Then complete the response.

I'm the same.	OR	I'm different.
1. ☐ Me neither. I don't like _____		☐ Really? I like _____
2. ☐ Me too. I really like _____		☐ Yeah? I don't like _____
3. ☐ I know. _____		☐ Really? I think _____

About you **C Pair work** Choose one of these situations. Make suggestions and choose a place to go together.

| *It's a beautiful day. Choose a place to sit in the sun.* | *It's Friday night. Choose a place to have some fun.* | *It's noon and you're hungry. Choose a place to eat together.* |

A Let's go somewhere and sit in the sun. It's a beautiful day.

B I know. Well, let's go to the park and get an ice cream.

Free talk p. 132

Lesson D / A neighborhood guide

1 Reading

A Do you know any neighborhoods with these things? Tell the class.

- unusual boutiques
- expensive jewelry stores
- comedy clubs
- poetry readings
- art galleries

B Read the website guide to a New York City neighborhood. What kinds of places are there? What do people do there?

Reading tip

Look at the photos in an article first. They can tell you what the article is about.

http://www.neighborhoodNY...

The Village

Welcome to Manhattan's Greenwich Village.

This "artsy" neighborhood has something for everyone. There are outdoor cafés, great theaters, music and comedy clubs, interesting stores, restaurants, and beautiful parks.

Bleecker Street shopping

Window-shopping on this busy street is fun. There are some wonderful stores and unusual boutiques. It's a great place to buy books, clothes, and jewelry. Stores are usually open between 11:00 a.m. and 8:00 p.m.

Washington Square Park

There are a lot of free events in this beautiful park – concerts, movies, poetry readings, and more! It's also the perfect place to just sit and enjoy some quiet time and maybe play a chess game. It's open from early morning to 1:00.

Live music in the Village

There's a great music "vibe" in the Village with street performers, old record stores, and the Village's famous jazz clubs, such as Fat Cat and the Blue Note. For more information about shows, visit the Gotham Jazz website at www.gothamjazz.com.

Art in the Village

The Village is full of art, and it's not just in the galleries. Check out this storefront covered in keys. Be sure to go to the Forbes Galleries. The exhibits change throughout the year, and there is always something new to see. The galleries are open Tuesday through Saturday, and admission is free.

Call the visitor hotline at 1-555-805-4040 for more information about New York City.

C Read the article again. Are these statements true or false? Check (✓) *True* (T) or *False* (F).

	T	F
1. Bleecker Street is a great place to go window-shopping.	☐	☐
2. Washington Square Park opens at one o'clock in the morning.	☐	☐
3. Washington Square Park has free galleries.	☐	☐
4. www.gothamjazz.com is a website with information on jazz clubs.	☐	☐
5. The Forbes Galleries are expensive.	☐	☐

2 Talk about it Exciting places

Group work Answer the questions below. Discuss your ideas. Agree on the best places.

What's . . .
a great place to shop?
a good place to find unusual clothes?
a fun place to go window-shopping?

Where's . . .
an "artsy" neighborhood?
a fun place to people watch?
a beautiful park?

What's . . .
a popular club?
a good place for live music?
a good place to see art exhibits?

Where's . . .
the best outdoor café?
an interesting museum?
an unusual building?

A *Shinjuku is the best place to shop. There are a lot of cool shops there.*
B *I know. But I think Ginza is the best place. It's expensive, but window-shopping is fun.*

3 Writing A neighborhood guide

A Choose a place to include in a neighborhood guide. Write down the information you need. Think about the questions below.

Where is it?	Why do you like it?	What time does it open and close?	Where can you get information?

B Read the Help note and then circle the prepositions in the neighborhood guide below.

Wilson Park

Wilson Park is a beautiful park (on) Green Street in Fairview. It's a great place to play sports. There's a soccer field, a couple of baseball fields, and some free tennis courts. There are free concerts at the stadium on the weekends. They start at 5:00 p.m. There's also a nice café, and it's open from 9:00 a.m. to 8:00 p.m., Tuesday through Sunday.

Call the Park Office at 686-555-2400 between 9:00 and 5:00 for more information.

> **Help note**
>
> **Prepositions**
> • *Wilson Park is **on** Green Street.*
> • *It's **in** Fairview.*
> • *Park hours are **from** 7:00 a.m. **to** 9:00 p.m.*
> • *Call **between** 9:00 and 5:00.*
> • *Concerts are **at** 5 p.m. **at** the stadium.*
> • *The park is open Tuesday **through** Sunday.*
> • *There are free concerts **on** the weekends.*
> • *Call the Park Office **at** 555-2400 **for** more information.*

About you **C** Write a neighborhood guide like the one above. Use your ideas from above to help you.

D Read your classmates' guides. Find an interesting place to go.

Vocabulary notebook / A time and a place . . .

Learning tip *Linking ideas*

Link ideas together. For example, you can link the time of day with the things you do.

1 When do you usually do these things each day? Write the times.

6:30 a.m.	get up		finish work / school
	eat breakfast		get home
	go to work / school		have dinner
	eat lunch		go to bed

2 Make a daily planner like the one below on your computer. What do you and your family usually do at different times?

On your own

Draw a clock face. Where are you at each time of the day? Write notes next to the hours.

Can Do! Now I can . . .

☑ I can . . .   ☐ I need to review how to . . .

- ☐ describe a neighborhood.
- ☐ ask for and tell the time.
- ☐ make suggestions.
- ☐ show I have something in common with someone.
- ☐ agree with someone.

- ☐ understand announcements about events.
- ☐ understand conversations about arrangements.
- ☐ read a travel guide.
- ☐ write a city travel guide.

1 That's not quite right.

Which of these sentences are true for you? Check (✓) *True* (T) or *False* (F).
Correct the false sentences.

	T	F			T	F
1. Our English class is in the morning.	☐	☑		6. We have a lot of homework.	☐	☐
2. I never come to class late.	☐	☐		7. The students sometimes eat in class.	☐	☐
3. We have class three times a week.	☐	☐		8. Our teacher drives a car to class.	☐	☐
4. There are 30 students in this room.	☐	☐		9. Cell phones often ring in class.	☐	☐
5. There's a coffee break at 10:30 a.m.	☐	☐		10. We go out to a club after class.	☐	☐

Our English class isn't in the morning.   **OR**   *Our English class is in the evening.*

2 How much do you know about your partner?

Complete the sentences to make guesses about a partner. Then ask your partner
questions to find out if you are right or wrong.

Your guesses: My partner . . .	Are your guesses . . . right?	wrong?
1. _doesn't read_ a lot of books.	☑	☐
2. _____ the news on TV every night.	☐	☐
3. _____ with his / her parents.	☐	☐
4. _____ an hour a day on the Internet.	☐	☐
5. _____ at 6:00 a.m. on the weekends.	☐	☐
6. _____ tennis very well.	☐	☐

A *Do you read a lot of books?*

B *No, I don't. But I read the news on the Internet.*

A *OK. I'm right about that. Do you . . . ?*

3 How well do you know your city?

Complete the chart. Then use the words to tell a partner five things
about your city. Does your partner agree?

Places in a city	Words to describe places
restaurant	expensive

Useful expressions

a couple of
some
a lot of
no

A *There are a lot of expensive restaurants in our city.*

B *Right, but they're not very good.*

4 Ask a question in two ways; answer more than *yes* or *no*.

A Write a second question for each question below. Start the second question with *I mean*.

1. What's your neighborhood like? *I mean, do you like it?*
2. How often do you text your friends? _____
3. What kinds of sports do you watch on TV? _____
4. What time do you get up on the weekends? _____
5. Who does the laundry at your house? _____

B **Pair work** Take turns asking and answering the questions. Say more than *yes* or *no* in your answers. Use *Well* if your answer isn't a simple *yes* or *no*.

A What's your neighborhood like? I mean, do you like it?
B Well, it's not exciting, but there are a lot of beautiful parks.

5 Are you the same or different?

A Unscramble the words to find eight kinds of TV shows.

ootrnac   *cartoon*   paso preoa   _____
mega whos _____   het senw   _____
scotmi   _____   elarity hosw _____
kalt oswh   _____   mucrtayenod _____

B **Pair work** Talk about your TV habits. Use *Me too* and *Me neither* if you're the same. Use *Really? . . .* if you're different.

A I never watch cartoons.
B Me neither. I don't like cartoons.   **OR**   *Really? I love cartoons.*

6 What's your routine?

Complete each question with a verb. Can you think of four more questions? Then ask and answer with a partner.

What time do you . . .	When do you . . .
have breakfast?	_____ time with your family?
_____ to work or to class?	_____ out with your friends?
_____ home at night?	_____ to the movies?
_____	_____

How often do you . . .	Where do you . . .
_____ at the gym?	_____ your homework?
_____ the subway or the bus?	_____ shopping?
_____ your email?	_____ lunch?
_____	_____

A What time do you have breakfast?
B I usually eat breakfast around seven o'clock.

UNIT 1 The name game

Group work Follow the instructions below. Continue the game until you know all the names of the students in your group.

Student A: Say your full name. If you have a middle name or nickname, say it.

Student B: Repeat Student A's name. Then say your name.

Student C: Repeat the names of the other students in your group.

Then say your name.

A *My full name is Rumiko Noguchi. I don't have a middle name or a nickname.*

B *OK. Your name is Rumiko Noguchi. My name is Carlos Sanchez. My nickname is Flaco.*

C *Your name is Carlos Sanchez. Your nickname is Flaco. And your name is Rumiko Noguchi . . .*

My full name is Rumiko Noguchi.

My nickname is Flaco.

UNIT 2 What do you remember?

1 Look at the picture. Where are the things in the room? Study the picture for two minutes and try to remember.

2 Pair work Close your books. Make a list of the things in the room and where they are. How much can you remember? Then open your books and check.

1. chair - next to the window
2. table - in front of the chair

A *The chair is next to the window.*

B *Right. And the table is in front of the chair.*

Free talk

  3 **Guess the famous person.**

Pair work Think of a famous living sports star, movie star, musician, or singer. Take turns asking your partner *yes-no* questions to guess the famous person he or she is thinking of. You can ask 10 questions!

A *Is the person female?*

B *No.*

A *Is he a sports star?*

B *Yes, he is.*

A *Is he a soccer player?* . . .

> **Useful language**
>
> Is the person male / female?
> Is he / she . . . ?
> - a sports star – a soccer player
> - a player for (name of the team)
> - an actor / a movie star
> - a singer / a rock star / in a band
> - a musician / a guitar player
>
> Is he / she . . . ?
> - married / single
> - old / young
> - an actor / a movie star
> - interesting / smart / funny
> - from China / from Turkey

UNIT **4** **Do you have the same media habits?**

Pair work Read these facts about young adults in the United States. Are you the same or different? How about your partner? Take turns asking questions. Write *S* for *Same* and *D* for *Different*.

	You	Your partner
97% of young adults use the Internet every day.		
83% use social networking sites.		
15% of young adults write blogs		
96% of young adults have a cell phone.		
66% have a smartphone.		
Young people spend only 20 minutes a day on phone calls.		
They send and receive an average of 110 text messages a day.		
They watch television two to three hours a day.		
81% use their phones and watch TV at the same time.		

A *Do you use the Internet every day?*

B *Yes, I do. I check my email every morning. How about you?*

A *Well, I check my email all day. So, yeah.*

UNIT **5** **Favorite free-time activities**

1 Make guesses about your partner. Write your guesses in the chart under *My guesses*.

	My guesses	My partner's answers
What does he / she usually do on weeknights?	*watches TV*	
What kinds of TV shows does he / she like?		
What's his / her favorite TV show?		
How often does he / she watch TV news?		
Does he / she sleep late on the weekends?		
What's his / her favorite weekend activity?		
How often does he / she go to the movies?		
What kinds of movies does he / she like?		
Does he / she play a sport?		
Does he / she ever go to clubs?		
Is he / she a good dancer?		
What does he / she do after class?		
What kinds of restaurants does he / she go to?		
Does he / she like shopping?		
What hobbies does he / she have?		

2 **Pair work** Take turns asking the questions in two ways to find out if your guesses were right. When you answer, use *I mean* to say something more.

A *What do you usually do on weeknights? Do you watch TV?*

B *Yeah, I do. I watch my favorite reality show. I mean, I don't watch TV every night. On the weekends, I go out and . . .*

UNIT
6 **Find the differences.**

1 **Pair work** Look at the two neighborhoods below. How many differences do you see? Make a list.

Washington Circle

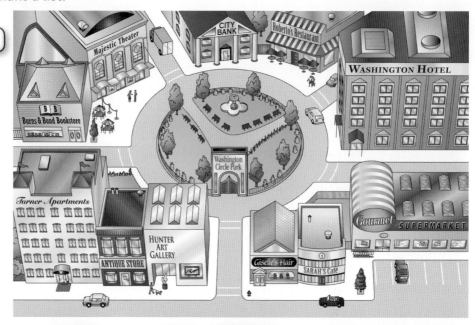

Lincoln Square

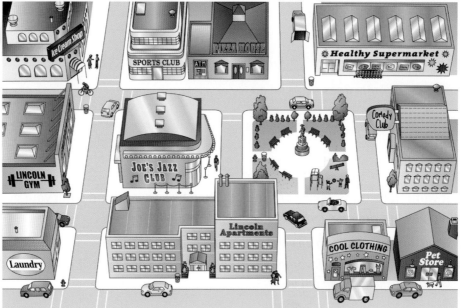

A *There's a big park in Washington Circle.*

B *There's a park in Lincoln Square, but it's very small. So that's one difference.*

Differences
1. *There's a big park in Washington Circle, but there's a small park in Lincoln Square.*

2 **Pair work** Discuss the things you like about the neighborhoods above. Are they like your neighborhood?

A *I like Washington Circle. It has a big park.*

B *Me too. There are a lot of parks in my neighborhood.*

UNIT **1** 🔊 **3.39** Listen and repeat the words. Notice the underlined sounds. Check (✓) the sounds that are like the sound in *hi*.

☑ 1. I'm ☐ 2. m**i**ddle ☐ 3. m**y** ☐ 4. n**i**ce ☐ 5. n**i**ckname ☐ 6. n**i**ght ☐ 7. w**ai**t

UNIT **2** 🔊 **3.40** Listen and repeat the words. Notice the underlined sounds. Are the sounds like the sound in *key* or the sound in *late*? Circle the correct word.

1. asl**ee**p (key / late)   4. th**e**se (key / late)
2. sh**e** (key / late)   5. th**ey** (key / late)
3. p**a**per (key / late)   6. tod**ay** (key / late)

UNIT **3** 🔊 **3.41** Listen and repeat the words. Notice the underlined sounds. Are the sounds like the sound in *see* or the sound in *zero*? Write *s* or *z*.

1. ama**z**ing _z_   4. it'**s** ____   7. **c**elebrity ____   10. **s**ister ____
2. bo**ss** _s_   5. bu**s**y ____   8. mu**s**ic ____   11. hi**s** ____
3. i**s** ____   6. la**z**y ____   9. ex**c**iting ____   12. **s**inger ____

UNIT **4** 🔊 **3.42** Listen and repeat the words. Notice the underlined sounds. Are the sounds like the sounds in *study*, *phone*, *get*, or *law*? Write the words from the box in the correct columns below.

br**ea**kfast   c**a**ll   c**o**ffee   c**ou**ntry   d**oe**s   **e**xercise   h**o**me   kn**ow**

study	phone	get	law
			coffee

UNIT **5** 🔊 **3.43** Listen and repeat the words. Notice the underlined sounds. Which sound in each group is different? Circle the odd one out.

1. d**o**cumentary   sitc**o**m   (m**o**vie)   sh**o**p
2. d**o**n't   **o**nline   g**o**   ph**o**to
3. c**o**mputer   tod**ay**   h**o**me   t**o**morrow
4. wh**o**   d**o**   t**oo**   c**o**mmercial

UNIT **6** 🔊 **3.44** Listen and repeat the words. Notice the underlined sounds. Which sound in each group is different? Circle the odd one out.

1. b**ui**lding   t**i**me   g**y**m   m**i**dnight
2. h**u**ngry   c**ou**ple   s**o**me   p**oo**l
3. m**o**vie   n**ew**   s**o**ccer   f**oo**d
4. m**a**ll   st**a**dium   **ei**ght   n**ei**ghborhood

UNIT 1 Lesson B The verb *be*: *I, you,* and *we*

A Complete the conversations with expressions from the box. You can use some expressions more than once. Then practice with a partner.

| Am I | Are you | Are we | I am | you are | we are | I'm | You're | We're |

1. Jennifer   Good morning. _____ here for a French class.

    Mrs. Lee   What's your last name, please?

    Jennifer   Gomes.

    Mrs. Lee   OK. _____ Silvia Gomez?

    Jennifer   No, _____ not. I'm Jennifer Gomes.

    Mrs. Lee   How do you spell *Gomes*?

    Jennifer   G-O-M-E-S.

    Mrs. Lee   Oh, OK. You're in French 2.

    Jennifer   Oh. _____ in Room B?

    Mrs. Lee   Yes, _____ . Oh, wait— you're not in Room B. _____ in Room A.

    Jennifer   Thank you. Have a nice day!

    Mrs. Lee   You too. Good-bye.

2. Drew   Hi. _____ here for a French class?

    Jennifer   Yes, _____ . My name's Jennifer. But everyone calls me Jen.

    Drew   Nice to meet you, Jen. _____ Drew.

    Jennifer   Drew?

    Drew   Yes. My full name is Andrew. Drew's my nickname.

    Jennifer   Oh, OK.

    Drew   Well, I'm in French 3, in Room B. _____ in the same class?

    Jennifer   No, we're not. I'm in Room A.

    Drew   Oh. _____ in different classes.

    Jennifer   Yes, _____ .

    Drew   Oh, well. . . . See you later, Jen.

    Jennifer   Yes. See you.

About you **B** **Pair work** Practice the conversations again. Use your own information.

UNIT 1 Lesson C *What's . . . ?; It's . . .*

A Complete the conversations. Use the questions in the box or write *It's*.

Am I in Room 2?	What's my teacher's name?	✓Are you a member?
How are you?	What's your email address?	What's your name?
How do you spell your last name?		

1. A   Hello. I'm here for a yoga class.

    B   Oh, OK. *Are you a member?*

    A   Um, yes.

    B   OK. Have a good class.

    A   Thank you. Oh, by the way. _____

    B   _____ Lucinda.

    A   OK. Thanks. Oh. _____

    B   Yes, you are. Room 2.

2. A   Good morning. _____

    B   I'm fine, thanks.

    A   Are you a new student? _____

    B   Um, yeah. _____ Anton Sokolov.

    A   _____

    B   S-O-K-O-L-O-V.

    A   OK. _____

    B   _____ anton@cup.org.

About you **B** **Pair work** Practice the conversations. Use your own information.

Extra practice

UNIT 2 **Lesson A** The verb *be*: *he*, *she*, and *they*

Complete the questions and answers. Then practice with a partner.

1. A Where's Hiroki? <u>*Is he*</u> absent?

   B No, _____ not. _____ right here.

2. A Stacy and Carmen are late today.

   B _____ at the library?

   A No, _____ not. _____ in the cafeteria.

3. A _____ Nick and Laura in class?

   B Yes, _____ . But _____ asleep.

4. A David's not here today.

   B _____ sick?

   A Yes, _____ . I think _____ at home.

> **✗ Common errors**
>
> Use *not* to make a statement negative. Don't use *no*.
>
> *Ellen's **not** here.*
> (NOT *Ellen's ~~no here~~. /*
> *~~Ellen no is here~~.*)

UNIT 2 **Lesson B** *This* and *these*; noun plurals

Rewrite items 1 to 3 in the plural and items 4 to 6 in the singular. Then compare with a partner.

1. Is this my key? – No, it's not.   <u>*Are these my keys? – No, they're not.*</u>
2. What's this? – It's a dictionary.   _____
3. This is a good sandwich!   _____
4. What are these? – They're tablets.   _____
5. My children aren't in class today.   _____
6. Are these your pencils? – Yes, they are. _____

UNIT 2 **Lesson C** Questions with *Where*; possessive *'s* and *s'*

Write questions using the words given. Then practice with a partner.

1. A <u>*Where's the teacher's coat?*</u>   (Where / the teacher / coat?)

   B It's on the chair.

2. A _____   (Where / the students / cafeteria?)

   B I think it's next to the library.

3. A _____   (Where / the teachers / room?)

   B It's right over there.

4. A _____   (Where / the students / test papers?)

   B Maybe they're in the desk.

5. A _____   (Where / the teacher / book bag?)

   B Look — it's under the desk.

UNIT 3 — Lesson A *Be* in statements; possessive adjectives

Complete the sentences. Compare with a partner. Then write four sentences about your favorite celebrities.

1. I'm not a soccer fan, but _____*I'm*_____ a big tennis fan. _____*My*_____ favorite player is Maria Sharapova.
2. My brother and I are baseball fans. _____ big fans of the New York Yankees.
3. My best friend and I are on the school baseball team. _____ team is very good this year.
4. My favorite band is One Direction. _____ really good. _____ new album is great.
5. I love Pablo Picasso. _____ my favorite artist. _____ paintings are amazing.
6. I like J. K. Rowling. She's my favorite writer. _____ very famous. _____ books are wonderful.

UNIT 3 — Lesson B *Yes-no* questions and answers; negatives

Write *yes-no* questions. Then write true answers. Ask and answer the questions with a partner.

1. you / shy ?
   A *Are you shy?*
   B *No, I'm not. I'm very outgoing.*

2. this class / easy ?
   A _____
   B _____

3. the teacher / strict ?
   A _____
   B _____

4. our classmates / lazy ?
   A _____
   B _____

5. your neighbors / nice ?
   A _____
   B _____

6. your best friend / outgoing ?
   A _____
   B _____

UNIT 3 — Lesson C Information questions with *be*

About you **Write questions for the answers below. Compare with a partner. Then ask and answer the questions giving your own information.**

1. A *Where's your mother today?*
   B My mother's at home today. She's sick.

2. A _____
   B It's my cousin. She's really nice.

3. A _____
   B My brother? He's friendly and outgoing.

4. A _____
   B My aunt and uncle are both fine.

5. A _____
   B My father's 50, and my mother's 48.

6. A _____
   B My grandfather's from Mexico City, and my grandmother's from Texas.

Extra practice

UNIT **4** **Lesson A** Simple present statements

A Complete the sentences. Use the simple present of the verbs in the box. Use affirmative verbs in items 1 to 4 and negative verbs in items 5 to 8.

> **Common errors**
>
> Add an **-s** ending to verbs with *he*, *she*, *it*, or singular nouns.
>
> He listen**s** to the radio. (NOT ~~listen~~...)
> My mom read**s**. (NOT ~~read~~.)

do	go (2)	like	play	sing	✓watch
eat	have	listen	talk	use	

1. It's very noisy in our house in the morning. My mother __watches__ TV.
2. My father _____ to the radio, and he _____ in the shower!
3. My brother _____ a new laptop, and he _____ computer games.
4. My sister's quiet. She _____ her homework and then _____ to school.
5. I _don't eat_ breakfast. I just have orange juice. I _____ coffee.
6. I have a big lunch at work with my best friend. We _____ home for lunch.
7. My friend is very quiet and shy. She _____ a lot at lunch.
8. I get up early on weekdays, but on the weekends I _____ an alarm clock.

About you **B** Pair work Rewrite five of the sentences above using your own information. Compare with a partner.

UNIT **4** **Lesson B** Yes-no questions and short answers

A Complete these questions with *do* or *does*, and the answers with *do, does, don't,* or *doesn't*. Then practice with a partner.

1. A ___Do___ you clean your room every day?
   B No, I _____. I only clean my room on Saturdays.

2. A _____ your teacher work on the weekends?
   B No, he _____. He only works on weekdays.

3. A _____ your friends text you late at night?
   B Yes, they _____. But they _____ call me late at night.

4. A _____ you watch TV with your family in the evenings?
   B No, we _____ watch TV together. We _____ like the same shows!

5. A _____ your mother go shopping on Saturdays?
   B Yes, she _____. But she _____ like shopping.

6. A _____ your family eat together on Sundays?
   B Yes, we _____. But we _____ eat at home. We go to my grandparents' house.

About you **B** Pair work Practice the conversations. Give your own information.

142

UNIT

5 **Lesson A** Simple present information questions

A Write a question about the underlined words in each answer. Then practice with a partner.

1. A *What do you do on Friday nights?*

   B On Friday nights? Oh, I usually go to the movies.

2. A _____

   B I go to the movies with my best friend.

3. A _____

   B My best friend texts me two or three times a day.

4. A _____

   B I have dinner with my parents on Sundays.

5. A _____

   B My parents live about 20 miles away.

6. A _____

   B My teacher? I guess she just goes home after class.

About you **B** **Pair work** Ask and answer the questions. Give your own information.

UNIT

5 **Lesson B** Frequency adverbs

A Answer the questions using frequency adverbs.

1. Do you ever go out on weeknights? *Well, sometimes I go out on Thursday nights.*
2. Do you ever go to the movies alone? _____
3. Do you ever exercise at a gym? _____
4. Do you ever play video games with your friends? _____
5. Do you ever study English with a classmate? _____
6. Do you ever read in bed? _____
7. Do you ever drink tea? _____
8. Do you ever have dinner late at night? _____

About you **B** **Pair work** Ask and answer the questions. Give your own information.

Extra practice

Lesson A *There's* and *There are*; quantifiers

A Cross out the incorrect words in this
email message.

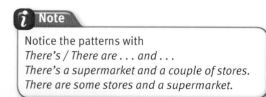

Note

Notice the patterns with
There's / There are . . . and . . .
There's a supermarket and a couple of stores.
There are some stores and a supermarket.

to: paul.renny@quickmail.net   attach

Hi, Paul!
I have **a / an** new apartment, and I love it. I'm in **a / an** exciting
neighborhood. **There's / There are** a cool jazz club and a couple
of nice outdoor cafés here. **There's / There are** also a beautiful
park and **a / an** amazing mall. In the mall, **there's / there are** two
expensive restaurants and a couple of nice outdoor **café / cafés**.
I go to the café! :) At the mall, there are a lot of **expensives /
expensive** stores, so I don't shop there. But there's **a / an** big
movie theater with a little café, so I hang out there sometimes.
Write soon.

Yours,
Megan

In conversation

There's is more common
than *There is*.

█████████ There's
████ There is

About you **B** **Pair work** Write an email about your neighborhood. Then compare emails with a partner.
How are your neighborhoods the same? How are they different?

Lesson B Suggestions with *Let's*

A Complete the sentences with *Let's* or *Let's not* and the verbs given.

1. _____ a break. (take) I know — _____ coffee
   at that new outdoor café! (have)

2. Class starts at 7:30 today. So _____ late. (not / be)

3. I know it's only 11:30, but I'm hungry! _____ lunch now. (eat)

4. _____ the laundry this afternoon. (not / do)
   _____ shopping at the mall. (go)

5. I feel tired. _____ tonight. (not / go out) _____ in front of the TV. (relax)

6. _____ for dinner tonight – say, around 7:30. (meet)

7. It's a beautiful day. _____ the house today. (not / clean)
   _____ to the pool! (go)

8. _____ Sunday afternoon at the museum. (spend) There's a great art exhibit there.

Note

Let's eat dinner now.
= I want dinner now.

Let's not eat dinner now.
= I don't want
  dinner now.

About you **B** Write five suggestions for things to do with your partner
this weekend. Then take turns making your suggestions.
Find something you both want to do.

In conversation

Let's is more common than *Let's not*.

Let's   Let's not

_____

_____

_____

Illustration credits

Harry Briggs: 5, 9, 14, 24, 31, 127, 129, 146 **©Cambridge University Press:** 6 *(leaf, left)*; 7 *(book, left)*; 25 *(heads)*; 54 *(building graphic, top right)*; 56 *(clocks, center)*; 100 *(calendar, background)*; 124 *(utensils, top left)* **Bunky Hurter:** 22, 32, 50, 86, 135 **Kim Johnson:** 10, 20, 30, 42, 52, 62, 74, 84, 96, 106, 116, 126 **Scott Macneil:** 54, 132 **Frank Montagna:** 12, 13, 19, 68, 79 **Q2A studio artists:** 119 **Gavin Reece:** 16, 46, 66, 120 **©Shutterstock:** 6 *(barcode, tree, airplane)*; 7 *(dumbbell, right)*; 44 *(clock, top left)*; 47 *(emoticons)*; 88 *(map)*, 92 *(map)*; 114 *(background)*; 115 *(background)* **Lucy Truman:** 6, 17, 26, 27, 34, 78, 118

Photography credits

Back cover: ©vovan/Shutterstock **8, 28, 29, 38, 39, 58, 59** ©Cambridge University Press **18, 19, 48, 49, 70, 71, 80, 81, 90, 91, 102, 103, 112, 113, 122, 123** ©Frank Veronsky **viii** *(left)* ©Design Pics/SuperStock; ©Aldo Murillo/istockphoto **1** *(clockwise from top left)* ©Don Hammond/MediaBakery; ©iofoto/Shutterstock; ©Tom Merton/MediaBakery **2** *(left)* ©Sigrid Olsson/Getty Images/RF; *(right)* ©Tetra Images/Getty Images/RF **3** *(left)* ©Photosindia/Alamy; *(right)* ©Fuse/Getty Images/RF **4** *(clockwise from left)* ©PT Images/Shutterstock; ©Monkey Business Images/Shutterstock; ©Chris Ryan/MediaBakery; ©Suprijono Suharjoto/istockphoto **6** *(left to right)* ©DV/MediaBakery; ©mangostock/Veer Images; ©Simon Greig/MediaBakery **9** *(left)* ©MediaBakery; ©Sam Edwards/MediaBakery **11** *(clockwise from top left)* ©l i g h t p o e t /Shutterstock; ©Fancy/MediaBakery; ©Rachel Frank/MediaBakery; ©Stockbroker/Alamy; ©Aleksandr Markin/Shutterstock **14** *(top row, left to right)* ©BEPictured/Shutterstock; ©nuttakit/Shutterstock; ©saginbay/Shutterstock; ©shutswis/Shutterstock; *(middle row, left to right)* ©Phant/Shutterstock; ©Julia Ivantsova/Shutterstock; ©Thinkstock; ©Anthony Berenyi/Shutterstock; *(bottom row, left to right)* ©Sergej Razvodovskij/Shutterstock; ©Hemera Technologies/Thinkstock; ©Julia Ivantsova/Shutterstock; ©ayazad/Shutterstock; ©Marc Dietrich/Shutterstock **15** *(top row, left to right)* ©Verdateo/Shutterstock; ©29september/Shutterstock; ©chaoss/Shutterstock; *(bottom row, left to right)* ©Stocksnapper/Shutterstock; ©dngood/MediaBakery; *(pens)* ©Elnur/Shutterstock; *(hand)* ©motorolka/Shutterstock **20** *(top row, left to right)* ©kate_sept2004/istockphoto; ©4kodiak/istockphoto; ©Kenneth C. Zirkel/istockphoto; ©ersinkisacik/istockphoto; ©Feng Yu/istockphoto *(bottom row, left to right)* ©Skip Odonnell/istockphoto; ©Kenneth C. Zirkel/istockphoto; ©Fancy Collection/SuperStock; ©Tobias Lauchenauer/istockphoto **21** *(clockwise from top left)* ©Lorenzo Santini/Stringer/Getty Images; ©Idealink Photography/Alamy; ©Karl Weatherly/MediaBakery; ©lev radin/Shutterstock; ©AHMAD FAIZAL YAHYA/Shutterstock; ©Kemter/istockphoto **22** *(clockwise from top left)* ©AF archive/Alamy; ©WireImage/Getty; ©Ken Durden/Shutterstock; ©Duncan Grove/Alamy **23** *(top to bottom)* ©ZUMA Press, Inc./Alamy; ©Michael Regan/Getty Images; ©Moviestore collection Ltd/Alamy; ©WireImage/Getty Images; ©DFree/Shutterstock **25** ©Slobodan Vasic/istockphoto **33** *(clockwise from top left)* ©Alejandro Rivera/istockphoto; ©zhang bo/istockphoto; ©Christopher Futcher/istockphoto; ©Helen King/Corbis; ©Rob Melnychuk/MediaBakery; ©MediaBakery **34** *(clockwise from top left)* ©Flashon Studio/Shutterstock; ©Hans Kim/Shutterstock; ©Jorg Hackemann/Shutterstock; ©Joana Lopes/Shutterstock **36** *(top row, left to right)* ©Chris Schmidt/istockphoto; ©JOSE LUIS PELAEZ/MediaBakery; ©TriggerPhoto/istockphoto *(bottom row, left to right)* ©londoneye/istockphoto; ©DrGrounds/istockphoto; ©Thinkstock **39** ©Holger Mette/istockphoto **40** ©Maartje van Caspel/istockphoto *(background)* ©J. Helgason/Shutterstock **41** ©Rouzes/istockphoto **43** *(clockwise from top left)* ©Jani Bryson/istockphoto; ©Steven Robertson/istockphoto; ©Thinkstock; ©MediaBakery **44** *(top to bottom)* ©Thinkstock; ©Thinkstock; ©Thinkstock; ©Stígur Karlsson/istockphoto **47** *(top row, left to right)* ©Cory Thoman/Shutterstock; ©Alan Diaz/AP/Corbis; ©Getty Images; ©Getty Images *(bottom row, left to right)* ©John Czenke/Shutterstock; ©CBS via Getty Images; ©Cliff Lipson/CBS via Getty Images; ©John Paul Filo/CBS via Getty Images **50** *(background)* ©URRRA/Shutterstock **51** *(left to right)* ©Neustockimages/istockphoto; ©Thinkstock **53** *(clockwise from top right)* ©Jeremy Enlow/MediaBakery; ©Getty Images; ©Medioimages/Photodisc/Thinkstock; ©Thinkstock **54** *(left to right)* ©Pressmaster/Shutterstock; ©auremar/Shutterstock; ©Andre Blais/Shutterstock **56** *(top row, left to right)* ©KtD/Shutterstock; ©Crisp/Shutterstock; ©Alex Staroseltsev/Shutterstock; ©Adam Radosavljevic/Shutterstock *(middle row, left to right)* ©Hayati Kayhan/Shutterstock; ©rdiraimo/istockphoto; ©Clayton Hansen/istockphoto; ©Jose Gil/Shutterstock *(bottom)* ©dwphotos/istockphoto **57** *(left to right)* ©Valua Vitaly/istockphoto; ©Thinkstock **60** *(clockwise from top left)* ©Patti McConville/Alamy; ©Kord/MediaBakery; ©2011 Scott Lynch/FlickrVision/Getty; ©Thinkstock **61** *(top, clockwise from top left)* ©Thinkstock; ©Andrii Gatash/istockphoto; ©Bill Varie/MediaBakery; ©Momcilo Grujic/istockphoto *(bottom)* ©Danger Jacobs/Shutterstock **62** *(phone)* © lculig/Shutterstock **63** ©Dmitriy Yakovlev/Shutterstock *(news)* ©Thinkstock **64** *(top to bottom)* ©Deklofenak/Shutterstock; ©Hill Street Studios/MediaBakery **65** *(clockwise from top left)* ©Superstock/RF; ©Sergiy Zavgorodny/istockphoto; ©Krzysztof Rafał Siekielski/istockphoto; ©AFP/Getty Images; ©VisualCommunications/istockphoto; ©Courtney Weittenhiller/istockphoto **67** ©Fotosearch/SuperStock **68** *(top row, left to right)* ©technotr/istockphoto; ©Image Source Plus/Alamy; ©ozgurcankaya/istockphoto *(middle row, left to right)* ©Bill Grove/istockphoto; ©mediaphotos/istockphoto; ©Andrew Rich/istockphoto *(bottom row, left to right)* ©Judi Ashlock/istockphoto; ©Thinkstock; ©MoniqueRodriguez/istockphoto **69** ©Design Pics/SuperStock **71** *(bottom)* ©Alan Look/Icon SMI/Newscom **72** *(top to bottom)* ©PATRICK LIN/AFP/Getty Images; ©Fabrice LEROUGE/MediaBakery *(background)* ©Shutterstock **73** *(left to right)* ©Bob Thomas/istockphoto; ©Thinkstock; ©ZUMA Wire Service/Alamy; ©DreamPictures/Getty Images/RF *(tablet computer)* ©Shutterstock **75** *(left to right)* ©Asia Images Group/Getty Images/RF; ©PhotoTalk/istockphoto; ©Holger Mette/istockphoto; ©Andrew Lever/istockphoto **76** *(left to right)* ©Izabela Habur/istockphoto; ©stocknroll/istockphoto; ©Justin Horrocks/istockphoto *(background)* ©Giuseppe Parisi/Shutterstock **78** *(top row, left to right)* ©angelo gilardelli/Shutterstock; ©FrameAngel/Shutterstock; ©Tatiana Popova/Shutterstock; ©Steve Collender/Shutterstock; ©Olena Zaskochenko/Shutterstock *(bottom row, left to right)* ©Cristian Baitg/istockphoto; ©kgfoto/istockphoto; ©Lutya/Shutterstock; ©Africa Studio/Shutterstock; ©Karkas/Shutterstock; ©nito/Shutterstock; ©Karkas/Shutterstock; ©Africa Studio/Shutterstock **81** *(red scarf)* ©kedrov/Shutterstock *(striped scarf)* ©dean bertoncelj/Shutterstock *(blue glasses)* ©Teeratas/Shutterstock; *(black glasses)* ©Africa Studio/Shutterstock *(striped socks)* ©Verkhovynets Taras/Shutterstock *(black socks)* ©shutswis/Shutterstock **82** *(left to right)* ©Maksym Bondarchuk/Shutterstock; ©Jochen Tack/Alamy **83** ©kzenon/istockphoto **85** *(clockwise from top left)* ©Prisma/SuperStock; ©Photononstop/SuperStock; ©Stock Connection/SuperStock; ©Prisma/SuperStock; ©Jon Arnold Images/SuperStock; ©Ingram Publishing/SuperStock **86** *(top to bottom)* ©Thinkstock; ©Frank van den Bergh/istockphoto; ©Jay Lazarin/istockphoto; ©Terraxplorer/istockphoto; ©Bernhard Richter/istockphoto **87** ©Arif Iqball/Alamy **88** ©Jacqueline Veissid/Getty Images/RF **89** *(top row, left to right)* ©Vinicius Tupinamba/Shutterstock; ©qingqing/Shutterstock; ©Duncan Hotston/istockphoto; ©Joe Gough/Shutterstock *(bottom row, left to right)* ©Harris Shiffman/istockphoto; ©sf_foodphoto/istockphoto; ©Piyato/Shutterstock; ©Janet Hastings/istockphoto **90** *(left to right)* ©Gregory Johnston/Shutterstock; ©Matej Michelizza/istockphoto; ©Food and Drink/SuperStock; ©Thinkstock **91** *(top)* ©Atlantide Phototravel/Corbis *(bottom, left to right)* ©Mariano Pozo/age fotostock/SuperStock; ©Stacey Gamez/istockphoto; ©Eric Tadsen/istockphoto; ©Eric Tadsen/istockphoto **92** *(clockwise from top left)* ©Robert Harding World Imagery/Alamy; ©Mordolff/istockphoto; ©fototrav/istockphoto; ©Nikada/istockphoto **93** *(top to bottom)* ©Travel Pictures Ltd/SuperStock; ©beboy/Shutterstock **97** *(clockwise from top left)* ©StockLib/istockphoto; ©Juice Images/SuperStock; ©age fotostock/SuperStock; ©Blend Images/SuperStock **98** *(clockwise from top left)* ©Darren Mower/istockphoto; ©Glow Images/SuperStock; ©AVAVA/Shutterstock; ©Blend Images/SuperStock; ©oleksa/Shutterstock; ©Elena Elisseeva/Shutterstock; ©Exactostock/SuperStock *(background)* ©Varga B. Virag/Shutterstock **100** *(top row, left to right)* ©Hill Street Studios/Blend Images/SuperStock; ©Stockbroker/SuperStock; ©Suprijono Suharjoto/istockphoto *(middle row, left to right)* ©Image Source/SuperStock; ©Image Source/SuperStock; ©Corbis/SuperStock *(bottom row, left to right)* ©Thinkstock; ©Stockbyte/Thinkstock; ©Radius/SuperStock **102** *(clockwise from top right)* ©zhang bo/istockphoto; ©Anna Bryukhanova/istockphoto; ©kali9/istockphoto Bryukhanova/istockphoto; © kali9/istockphoto **104** *(background)* ©stavklem/Shutterstock **105** *(background)* ©stavklem/Shutterstock **107** *(clockwise from top left)* ©Cusp/SuperStock; ©Leigh Schindler/istockphoto; ©Blue Jean Images/SuperStock **108** *(clockwise from top left)* ©LAWRENCE MIGDALE/Getty Images; ©eyedear/Shutterstock; ©Jupiterimages/Thinkstock; ©Kenneth Wiedemann/istockphoto *(background)* ©Africa Studio/Shutterstock **109** ©kim stillwell/istockphoto **110** ©Troels Graugaard/istockphoto **111** *(top row, left to right)* ©S. Kuelcue/Shutterstock; ©Nikki Bidgood/istockphoto; ©vilainecrevette/istockphoto *(bottom row, left to right)* ©Stockbroker/SuperStock; ©Thomas_EyeDesign/istockphoto; ©Queerstock, Inc./Alamy **114** ©Amanda Rohde/istockphoto **115** *(left to right)* ©Fancy Collection/SuperStock; ©Flirt/SuperStock **117** *(clockwise from top left)* ©oksix/Shutterstock; ©Tetra Images/SuperStock; ©FoodCollection/SuperStock; ©Maria Komar/Shutterstock; ©Robyn Mackenzie/Shutterstock; ©Exactostock/SuperStock; ©Foodfolio/Photocuisin/Photocuisine/SuperStock **120** *(spinach)* ©Hong Vo/Shutterstock; *(onions and garlic)* ©Ilja Generalov/Shutterstock; *(peppers)* ©Ruslan Kuzmenkov/Shutterstock; *(green beans)* ©Andrey Starostin/Shutterstock; *(lettuce)* ©Kasia Bialasiewicz/Shutterstock; *(tomatoes)* ©Kelvin Wong/Shutterstock; *(oil)* ©undrey/Shutterstock; *(butter)* ©TRINACRIA PHOTO/Shutterstock; *(mangoes)* ©Svetlana Kuznetsova/Shutterstock; *(melon)* ©Thinkstock; *(strawberries)* ©photastic/Shutterstock; *(apples)* ©Loskutnikov/Shutterstock; *(pineapple)* ©Valentina Proskurina/Shutterstock; *(coffee)* ©Valentyn Volkov/Shutterstock; *(sugar)* ©Food and Drink/SuperStock; *(tea)* ©Anastasios71/Shutterstock; *(potato chips)* ©Aerostato/Shutterstock; *(cereal)* ©Mikhail hoboton Popov/Shutterstock; *(peanuts)* ©Drozdowski/Shutterstock; *(cookies)* ©endeavor/Shutterstock; *(ice cream)* ©neiromobile/Shutterstock; *(lamb)* ©Gregory Gerber/Shutterstock; *(shrimp)* ©Flashon Studio/Shutterstock; *(salmon)* ©Enshpil/Shutterstock; *(hamburger meat)* ©OlegD/Shutterstock **124** *(top to bottom)* ©AFP/Getty Images; ©AP Photo/Lionel Cironneau; ©SUKREE SUKPLANG/REUTERS/Newscom **125** ©Atlantide Phototravel/Corbis *(tablet computer)* ©Shutterstock **128** *(top to bottom)* ©Ryan McVay/Thinkstock; ©Pete Saloutos/istockphoto **129** *(left to right)* ©akiyoko/istockphoto; ©Thinkstock **131** ©sturti/istockphoto **134** *(top row, left to right)* ©David Pedre/istockphoto; ©Ricardo De Mattos/istockphoto *(middle row, left to right)* ©Alija/istockphoto; ©vario images GmbH & Co.KG/Alamy *(bottom row, left to right)* ©Steve Vidler/SuperStock; ©Prisma Bildagentur AG/Alamy **135** ©Thinkstock **136** *(left to right)* ©Lisa-Blue/istockphoto; ©Alexander Raths/istockphoto

Text credits

While every effort has been made, it has not always been possible to identify the sources of all the materials used, or to trace the copyright holders. If any omissions are brought to our notice, we will be happy to include the appropriate acknowledgements on reprinting.